Santa Fe Art Colony, 1900–1942

Artists

Jozef G. Bakos (1891–1977)

Cyrus L. Baldridge (1889–1975)

Henry C. Balink (1882–1963)

Gustave Baumann (1881–1971)

Homer Boss (1882–1956)

Paul Burlin (1886–1969)

Gerald Cassidy (1879–1934)

Andrew Dasburg (1887–1979)

Randall Davey (1887–1964)

Fremont Ellis (1897–1985)

Marsden Hartley (1877–1943)

William Penhallow Henderson (1877–1943)

Robert Henri (1865–1929)

Russel Vernon Hunter (1900–1955)

Raymond Jonson (1891–1982)

Gina Schnaufer Knee (1898–1982)

Alfred G. Morang (1901–1958)

Lloyd Moylan (1893–1963)

Willard Nash (1898–1943)

B. J. O. Nordfeldt (1878–1955)

Sheldon Parsons (1866–1943)

Warren E. Rollins (1861–1962)

Julius Rolshoven (1858–1930)

William Howard Shuster (1893–1969)

John Sloan (1871–1951)

Theodore Van Soelen (1890–1964)

Carlos Vierra (1876–1937)

Cady Wells (1904–1954)

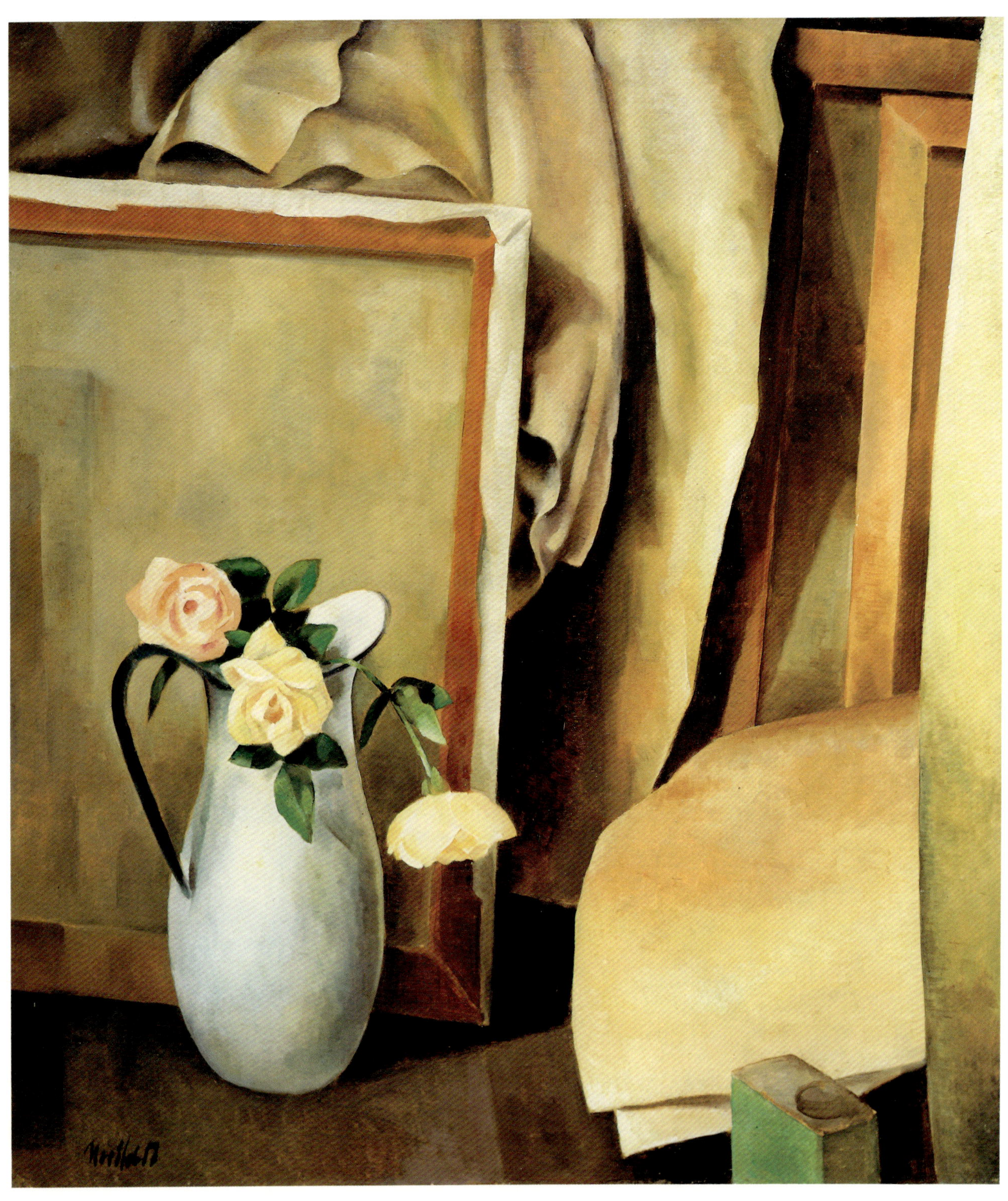

B. J. O. Nordfeldt, *Roses and Canvas,* c. 1930–31, oil on canvas, 34 × 30 in.

❧ Santa Fe Art Colony, 1900–1942 ❧

Sharyn Rohlfsen Udall

July 17–August 8, 1987

Gerald Peters Gallery, Santa Fe, New Mexico

Santa Fe Art Colony, 1900–1942
Sharyn Rohlfsen Udall
July 17–August 8, 1987
Gerald Peters Gallery, Santa Fe, New Mexico

Exhibition and catalog coordinated by Julie Schimmel
Editor: Nancy Pierson
Photography: Warren Hanford
Design: Eleanor Morris Caponigro
Typesetting: G & S Typesetters, Inc., Austin
Printing: Columbine Printing, Taos
Binding: Roswell Bookbinding, Phoenix

Cover: Fremont Ellis, *El Caballero,* oil on canvas,
        60 × 72 in.

Appreciation is extended to Abbeville Press, New York,
and the National Museum of American Art, Smithsonian Institution, for their permission to reprint por-
tions of the chronology which appeared in *Art in New
Mexico, 1900–1945: Paths to Taos and Santa Fe.*

Contents

Preface

Santa Fe today exceeds Taos in both general population and numbers of artists, yet the transformation of Taos from frontier town to artists' colony is the better known story. This catalog and the exhibition it accompanies, Santa Fe Art Colony, 1900–1942, is a first step to remedying the scarcity of material on Santa Fe's early artists, galleries, art schools, and museums.

The captured facts and shared perceptions that Sharyn Udall brings to this history of Santa Fe are not intended to push New Mexico further into a regional corner. Much that happened in the Southwest reflected trends that were national in scope. As New Mexico built its first museum in 1917, so did many other states across the country, spurred by the success of fine arts museums built in Boston and New York as early as the 1870s; as two art colonies flourished here, so did they in Connecticut, Maine, Massachusetts, New York, and Pennsylvania. And as New Mexico artists were painting murals in hotels, universities, and public buildings, so were artists across the country.

Yet, while New Mexico reflected national trends, it could also claim unique and special achievement. Few museums established poli-cies as liberal as those of the Museum of New Mexico, where studio space and unjuried exhibitions made artistic life a little easier, and where art, history, and science were equally nourished. Also, few art colonies existed as long or claimed as many permanent residents as those of New Mexico. Additionally, isolation led to innovative marketing schemes, and the Taos Society of Artists, followed in Santa Fe by Los Cinco Pintores and the New Mexico Painters, cultivated patrons across the country through traveling exhibitions organized by members.

The list of painters represented in this exhibition just touches on the number of artists who actually worked in Santa Fe. The paintings found in this catalog and exhibition are the result of prolonged scouting, yet there are many more to be discovered. We hope that this exploration will lead to additional paintings and research materials that will give greater insight yet into the city known, yet only partially explored.

Julie Schimmel
Director of Research
Gerald Peters Gallery

Let the Years Worry

Art Life in Santa Fe 1900–1942

The fast travelers with extra tires come in a hurry
and solve me and pass on to say all their lives,
"Santa Fe, oh yes, Santa Fe, I have seen Santa Fe."
"Hurry up," is their first and last word on my zigzag
streets, my lazy 'dobe corners.
"Hurry up, we must see the Old Church, the Old
    Bell, the
Oldest House in the United States, touch the doors,
and then go on — hurry up!"

These words may evoke Santa Fe in the 1980s, but it was sixty years ago that Carl Sandburg first visited and wrote this stanza in "Santa Fe Sketches." The tourist he wrote of might well have been found in Candelario's The Original Old Curio Store, which is still operating today as the Original Trading Post (fig. 1). However, Sandburg's muse caught sight of more than just the fast traveler:

The Valley was swept with a blue broom to the west,
there are blue broom leavings on the sky,
hangover blue wisps.
The valley city sits with its thoughts.
"Have I not had my thoughts by myself
four hundred years?" she asks.
"Do you wonder I sit here, shrewd, faded,
asking: What next? who next?
And answering: I don't care — let the years worry."[1]

Sandburg felt keenly the contradictory nature of three-hundred-year-old Santa Fe, a janus-faced town savoring its antiquity while trying to make some sense of the twentieth century. Unlike the hurried tourists trying to "solve" Santa Fe in a matter of hours or days, he saw the tourist consciousness of the place but felt, too, the pull of its austere beauty. In Santa Fe, tradition — antiquity and nature — and progress have been constant, if uneasy, companions, attracting every variety of visitor: health seeker, entrepreneur, dilettante, sightseer, and artist. It is the artist who has perhaps been most forced to reconcile unspoiled beauty with progress, to find a way to live and work that is both spiritually satisfying and financially rewarding. Much has been written about the lure of New Mexico, as Sandburg had written — of clean-swept skies, the restorative climate, penetrating light, and the grandeur of mountains shimmering in crystalline air. But what was it like to be a professional painter in Santa Fe in the first half of the twentieth century? Having succumbed to its natural charms, how did an artist without independent means earn a livelihood?

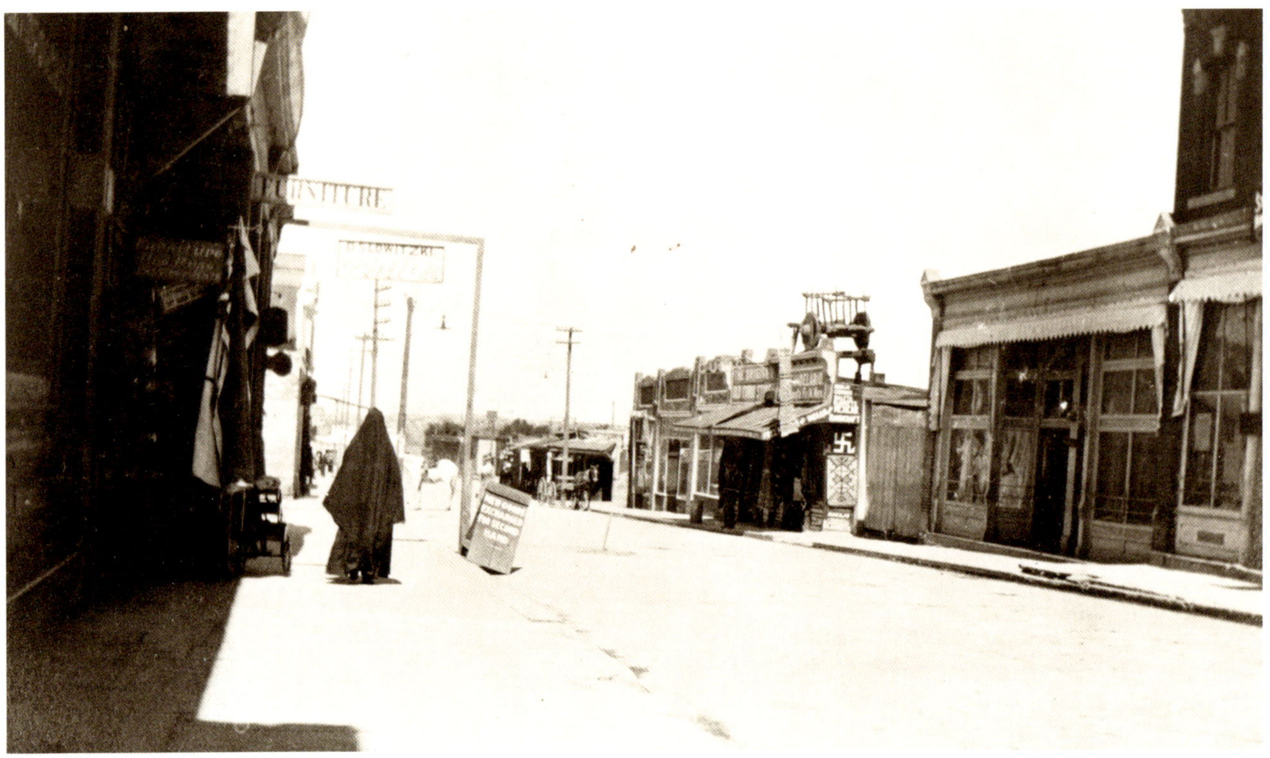

Fig. 1. San Francisco Street, Santa Fe, New Mexico, c. 1915. The building on the right with a cart is Candelario's The Original Old Curio Store.

Surely a town of fewer than seven thousand residents could not support a community of year-round artists, which by 1921 numbered fifteen or so. Despite the claim—which one doubts—that "in time almost every home in Santa Fe displayed original art," the locals could scarcely absorb the continuous production of a busy, hungry group of artists.[2] Obviously they had to expand their audience.

Many painters did have connections with cities at least as significant as those in Santa Fe. Among the early group, Julius Rolshoven had painted for eleven years in Florence, becoming well known for his Italian landscapes and acquiring a clientele in portraiture. When the Rolshovens arrived in New Mexico during World War I, they brought not only trunks full of sophisticated traveling clothes; their "baggage" also included his international reputation and the knowledge that buyers waited in the East for his colorful, romantic, southwestern scenes. Robert Henri relied on distant sources of income as well. His robust, realist style and reputation for brash innovation contrasted strongly with the sedate Rolshoven, but both found a warm welcome in New Mexico. Henri said of Santa Fe, "Here painters are treated with that welcome and appreciation that is supposed to exist only in certain places in Europe."[3]

There were additional artists who, despite frequent or sustained visits to New Mexico, retained exhibition and sales outlets outside New Mexico. Henri's pupil and protégé John Sloan was a vital member of the artistic community for some thirty years. Nonetheless, he found it necessary to market most of his southwestern subjects through New York galleries. Cyrus L. Baldridge visited Santa Fe frequently after his initial visit in 1926, but he had a worldwide market for his paintings as well as for written accounts of his travels. Paul Burlin and Andrew Dasburg, members of the New York avant-garde, had a foot in both the West and the East. Burlin spent much time in Santa Fe between 1913 and 1920 but maintained close ties to New York. Dasburg, who began in 1918 to visit New Mexico nearly every year, chose not to settle permanently in the Southwest until 1933. His New York and Woodstock connections remained vital to his livelihood during those years.

Over the next several decades New York would furnish Santa Fe with many artists. Chicago also sent its share, including B. J. O. Nordfeldt and Raymond Jonson. Gustave Baumann left Chicago for his health, William Penhallow Henderson for his wife's. Over the years many Santa Fe painters — Carlos Vierra, Sheldon Parsons, Gerald Cassidy, Theodore Van Soelen, Will Shuster, Alfred Morang — enlisted New Mexico's dry climate in their battles with lung ailments.

But did Santa Fe offer these artists, whose base shifted to the Southwest, financial and cultural sustenance? Unquestionably, the greatest source of support was the Museum of New Mexico. From its founding in 1909 until the Fine Arts building opened in 1917, the museum shared space in the old Palace of the Governors with the School of American Archaeology and the Historical Society of New Mexico. Few states could claim an institution as progressive in its thinking as the Museum of New Mexico, which freely extended studio and exhibition space to artists; combined art, history, and science; and collected both historical and contemporary art.

The museum began early having shows of Santa Fe artists. In 1916, despite the poorly lighted, crowded space of the Governor's Palace, it hung what was called the "second annual exhibit" of the "Santa Fe Artist Colony."[4] Probably not an organized group, these artists included Vierra, Parsons, Cassidy, Henri, and Henderson. Edgar L. Hewett, director of the school and the museum, made an effort to attract artists to Santa Fe. He had already provided some of these painters with free temporary studio space, complete with skylights, in the old Palace building. Over the years many artists accepted this welcoming gesture, including Rollins, Rolshoven, Burlin, Henri, Marsden Hartley, Dasburg, Randall Davey, and Willard Nash, as well as Pueblo Indians Ma-Pe-Wi, Crescencio Martinez, Awa Tsireh, and Pueblo-Hopi Fred Kabotie.

While Hewett viewed art as Santa Fe's incipient growth industry, not all Santa Feans shared his culture-boosterism. In 1915 Colonel José D. Sena, president of the local school board, questioned both the ultimate value of art to the town and the need for Hewett's proposed art museum. In a letter to the *Santa Fe New Mexican* Sena asked,

How many of the children of our city would become artists and derive benefit from the art gallery? Are you not aware that an exceedingly small percentage of the citizens of this great government of ours can and do dedicate themselves to art, and then those that dedicate themselves to that profession, many of them become subjects of the poorhouse?[5]

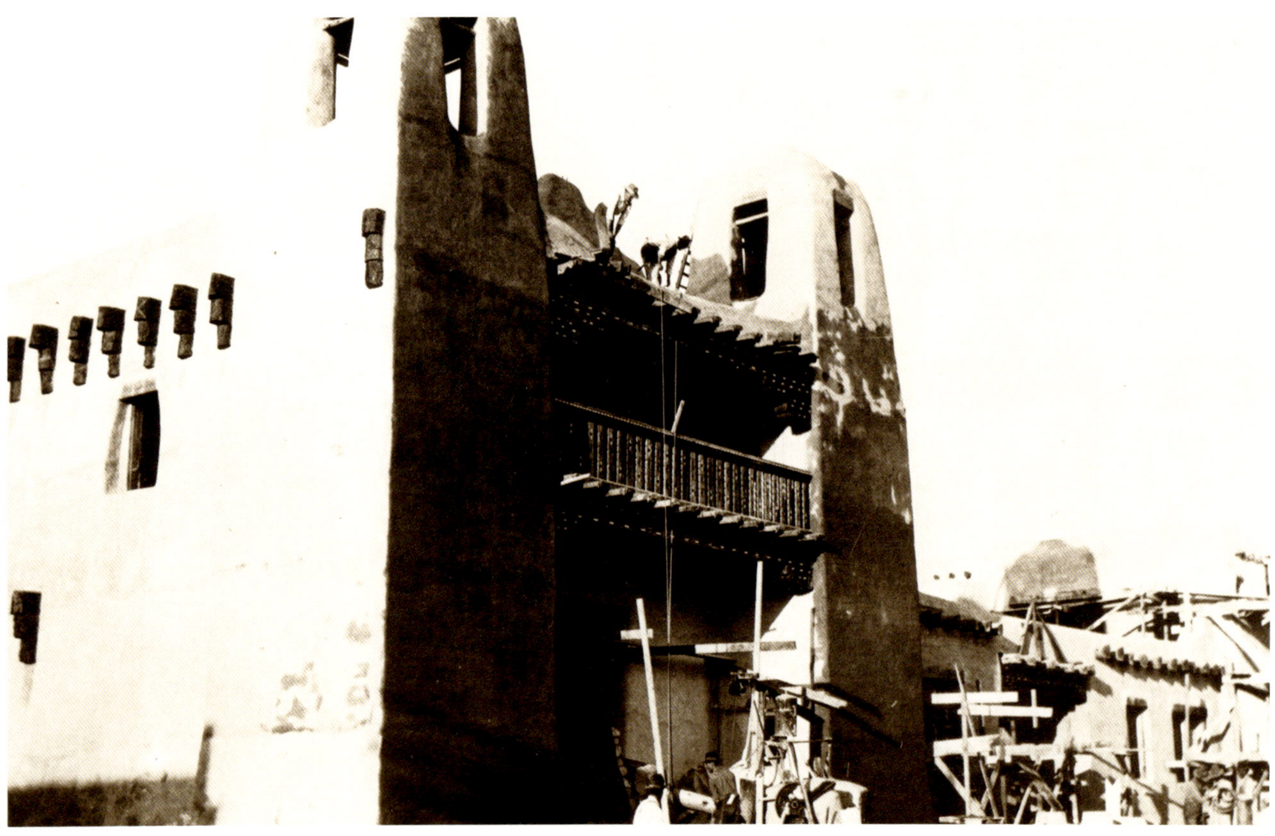

Fig. 2. St. Francis Auditorium, Fine Arts Museum, Santa Fe, New Mexico, under construction, c. 1917.

But Sena's objections were overridden and construction began on the building that was to be a landmark of the Spanish-Pueblo architecture so touted by Hewett, Vierra, and architect John Gaw Meem (fig. 2).

Once the new museum opened in 1917, its much greater exhibition space allowed artists easier and more frequent access to the public. Individual and group shows continued, encouraged by the liberal open-door exhibition policy heartily endorsed by Henri and Sloan in the early years of the new museum's operation. Declared Hewett, "The Museum extends its privileges to all who are working with a serious purpose in art."[6] This popular policy endured until 1951, when the sheer number of artists seeking exhibition space forced the museum to initiate a jury procedure for certain of its exhibits.

The museum scheduled its annual group show of Santa Fe artists for September to coincide with the revived Santa Fe Fiesta, a celebration commemorating the seventeenth-century Spanish reconquest of Santa Fe. In the 1921 program of the "Eighth Annual Exhibition by the Santa Fe Artists," the redoubtable Director Hewett, never given to understatement, wrote of Santa Fe's emerging cultural preeminence: "It is sometimes spoken of as the intellectual capital of the Southwest — to its region what Alexandria was to its age."[7] Regional chauvinism? Decidedly — but Hewett's pride was earnest, and his words, if exaggerated, were pro-

14

phetic. Yet most Santa Fe painters, despite the museum's help, were still unable to support themselves with local sales.

The Taos Society of Artists, organized in 1915, provided Santa Fe artists with a model for circulating and selling its members' paintings outside the state.[8] While the efforts of the Taos artists to find markets are well documented, those of Santa Fe artists are less so. The Santa Fe Arts Club, organized with the broadly stated aim of encouraging southwestern art, met in April 1922 to plan circulating exhibits. President Warren Rollins (then sixty-one) and Vice President Will Shuster (age twenty-nine) represented the town's long-established and recently arrived artists, respectively. Although the Arts Club was not to be a commercial success and Shuster soon channeled his effort into a smaller, more homogeneous group, the Arts Club remained to function as a cultural clearing house. The Club included music, literature, and drama sections, and its members participated officially or unofficially in many civic events. For example, in 1921 the Club organized New Year's Day festivities that included—with a bow to ubiquitous Art—a pageant "symbolizing the three primary colors."[9] One wonders how this pageant was received by the public. Less esoterically, the group organized artists' receptions and sponsored visiting speakers.

The group to which Shuster gravitated was Los Cinco Pintores, formed in 1921 by five recently arrived artists, all under age thirty. Jozef Bakos and Wladyslaw (Walter) Mruk came from Buffalo to Santa Fe by way of Denver, where they studied with painter John E. Thompson. Fremont Ellis left a fledgling career as an optometrist in El Paso to paint full time in Santa Fe. Shuster came on the recommendation of his teacher, Sloan. Among them, only Willard Nash, fresh from Detroit, had some economic stability, provided by a patron back in Michigan.

What the Arts Club had only contemplated Los Cinco Pintores quickly accomplished: In the fall of 1921 and 1922 they exhibited as a group in the museum's Fiesta show. Late in 1922 they circulated paintings to the Midwest, the following year to Los Angeles, and in 1924 to El Paso. Their small number enabled the Cinco to act quickly; their financial circumstances demanded it.

The museum was generous with its exhibition space, but Santa Fe in the early 1920s had almost no commercial gallery space. The five young artists therefore found it necessary to create their own sales opportunities. In 1923 they initiated a series of weekly exhibits and receptions held in their homes.[10] The first was scheduled for the Bakos residence, one of the string of adobes the artists constructed for themselves along Camino del Monte Sol. Nearby lived the Hendersons, the Dasburgs, and Frank Applegate, all offering friendly encouragement.

Home exhibitions were to be only temporary, however. In 1923 Los Cinco Pintores announced their plans to "build a gallery this summer, the artists performing the labor with their own hands, one third of the proceeds from the sale of all pictures to be set aside to pay for the material."[11] Theirs would be a true cooperative venture—one requiring mutual trust, shared energy, and unanimity of purpose. One wonders what became of the ambitious plan. Were too few paintings sold to purchase materials? Were the artists too busy painting to build? ("Less talk and more painting," suggested Shuster.[12]) Or did other exhibition avenues open? Certainly the Los Angeles Museum show gave their work out-of-state exposure, while the local museum continued to give them individual space.

But a more significant deterrent to the building plan may have been the formation in 1923 of still another artists' group: the New Mexico Painters. These Taos and Santa Fe artists intended to exhibit their work in major market centers and did so with their first tour to Boston and New York. The Santa Fe contingent included Nordfeldt, Baumann, and Bakos (Bakos also continued to exhibit with Los Cinco Pintores until 1926, when they disbanded). Membership expanded in 1924 to include Dasburg, Davey, Van Soelen, and Sloan at the time of the second exhibition, which toured to a wider audience than Los Cinco Pintores ever had. From 1923 to 1928, the New Mexico Painters remained an active entity, providing a showcase in major galleries and museums for some of New Mexico's more progressive artists.[13]

Every few years, loosely organized artists regrouped. In 1927 Bakos and Nash of Los Cinco Pintores joined Dasburg, Nordfeldt, Jonson, and Denver artist John Thompson to exhibit at the East-West Gallery in San Francisco. They called themselves simply "Six Men" and showed together the following year in Seattle, Los Angeles, and Tucson.

But such enterprising exhibition schemes, if satisfying in exposure, were often wanting in monetary return. Especially in Santa Fe, the prices painters received for their work often lagged behind escalating living expenses. When local artists staged in 1923 a benefit for drought-stricken Pueblos, the sale of fif-teen paintings brought only fifteen dollars apiece.[14] A lucky private sale might net a few hundred dollars, but often it seemed that Colonel Sena's gloomy assessment was all too accurate. On one early occasion only a hastily commissioned portrait by a prominent local citizen enabled Shuster to pay a hospital bill and bring home his wife and newborn son.

For most artists, Santa Fe continued to be a difficult place to earn a living. Henry Balink remarked, only half-jokingly, that "prices are figured according to altitude. That's why everything here is so high."[15] Actually, Santa Fe had been regarded as an inexpensive place to live before 1920. Marsden Hartley came to New Mexico partially to escape high living costs in the East. Yet by the time the Sloans purchased a house in 1920, the modest influx of tourists and artists had begun to drive up prices. Sloan remarked, "Wherever the artists go, the prices go up. . . . When we first went to Gloucester [1914] we could have bought two lots right on the water for less than we paid for our adobe house in Santa Fe."[16] Yet Sloan spent eight months of the year in New York, where his gallery sales and teaching produced the bulk of his annual income. Those who stayed in Santa Fe looked for closer help.

Many painters were forced to rely on other skills to supplement meager earnings. Bakos, Nordfeldt, and Henderson were skilled furniture designers and builders. Jonson sold painting supplies to his colleagues; Henderson practiced architecture. Bakos augmented his income for a time by making frames for the more affluent Randall Davey. Yet even Davey, whose portrait commissions were his bread and butter, felt the economic pinch. He mused, perhaps a bit wistfully,

16

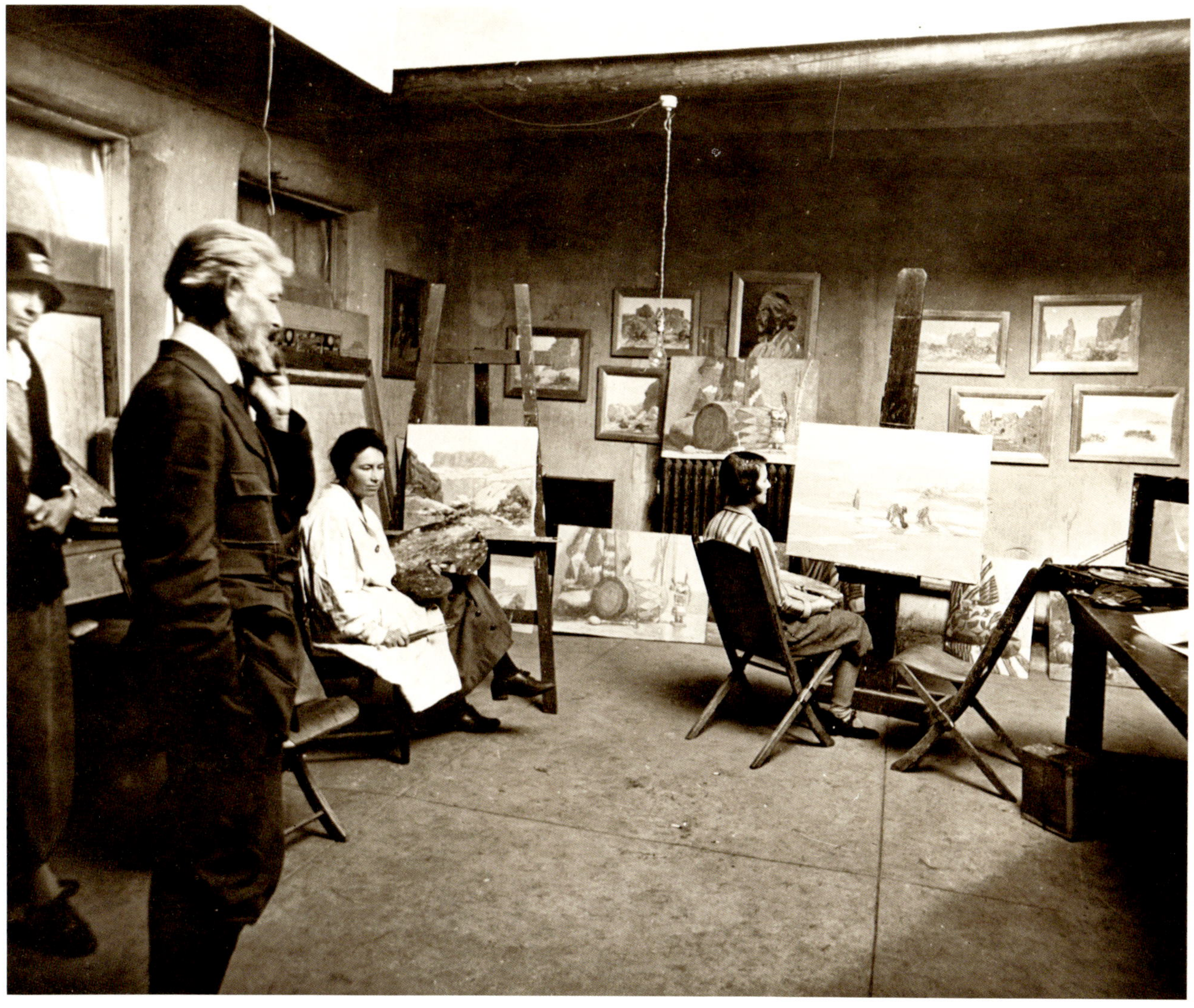

Fig. 3. Warren E. Rollins teaching painting in his studio, Palace of the Governors, Santa Fe, New Mexico, c. 1910.

If I lived in a big city I could clean up on portraits. But I prefer to live here and paint for myself, and get along with teaching, now and then a portrait commission, and with what little comes in from raising chickens.[17]

Surely Davey's tongue was in his cheek when he tossed in the chicken-raising reference. He managed, in reduced circumstances, to retain his membership in prestigious New York clubs, support a string of polo ponies, and live a life filled with music and books in his secluded Upper Canyon Road home. Compared with most Santa Fe painters, his was a luxurious, genteel existence.

Like Davey and other artists across America, more and more Santa Fe painters turned to teaching. It allowed them to work within their field and offered a cash income, often with some useful publicity and prestige thrown in. A number of painters brought teaching experience with them to the Southwest. Even today Henri and Sloan are best

17

remembered as teachers in Philadelphia and New York. Davey had taught with Henri in Spain, and in the United States beginning in 1912. During the twenties, Davey taught regularly at the Kansas City Art Institute and, along with Lloyd Moylan, at the Broadmoor Art Academy in Colorado Springs. Dasburg taught periodically in Woodstock and New York after 1917; Nordfeldt and Henderson had taught in Chicago. Of Los Cinco Pintores, Bakos had been an art instructor at the University of Colorado, and Ellis had done some teaching in El Paso. In the early years, one of the few teaching opportunities in Santa Fe was an occasional art class given through the museum, where Rollins taught (fig. 3). Andrew Dasburg often gave private instruction, working with Willard Nash in the twenties and Cady Wells in the thirties.

Summer art schools are central to the history of American art colonies, but not until 1925 did Santa Fe have its first art school. That year the Chappell School of Art, associated with the Denver Art Museum, announced the establishment of a summer branch in Santa Fe. Appointed to its directorship was Denver painter John Thompson. Thompson hired as teachers former pupils Mruk and Bakos as well as Dasburg, Nordfeldt, and Frank Applegate. He also asked Kenneth Chapman, a painter and member of the Museum of New Mexico staff, to teach a complementary course in southwestern Indian art. Nordfeldt assumed the director's position when Thompson's duties with the Denver Art Museum interfered. Classes, scheduled from mid-June to mid-September, were held in a vacant church at 415 West San Francisco Street. In addition to regular classes, the school sponsored painting expe-

ditions to nearby pueblos, mission churches, and cliff dwellings.

The Museum of New Mexico journal, *El Palacio,* was delighted with the prospect of an art school in town, remarking that while Santa Fe boasted more than twenty artists, none could previously be persuaded to give time to teaching.[18] One suspects they had never been offered the chance.

Annual Chappell summer sessions continued for three years, during which time the Denver Art Museum built its own collection of Indian and Hispanic art, much of it from New Mexico sources. When the school cancelled its 1928 Santa Fe season, *El Palacio* implied that a small artistic rivalry had been the cause: there would be no Chappell courses offered in Santa Fe "because of Denver's ambition to build up its own culture center."[19] It seems that both Denver and Santa Fe recognized the value of a summer art school. Besides attracting students from a wide geographic area, it also provided jobs for local artists.

For a time, there were two art schools in Santa Fe. Raymond Jonson competed with the Chappell School during its second year of operation, when he opened Atalaya Art School and conducted ten-week summer sessions in 1926 and 1927. When teaching, Jonson could frequently be found before the subject of the day with his students, as pictured here at the Santuario de Chimayo (fig. 4).

Disappointed Santa Feans lost no time in filling the void left by the Chappell School's departure. The Santa Fe Art School opened its doors under the directorship of painter-critic Cyril Kay-Scott the same year the Chappell Art School closed. Support for the school came from a strong local board of art-

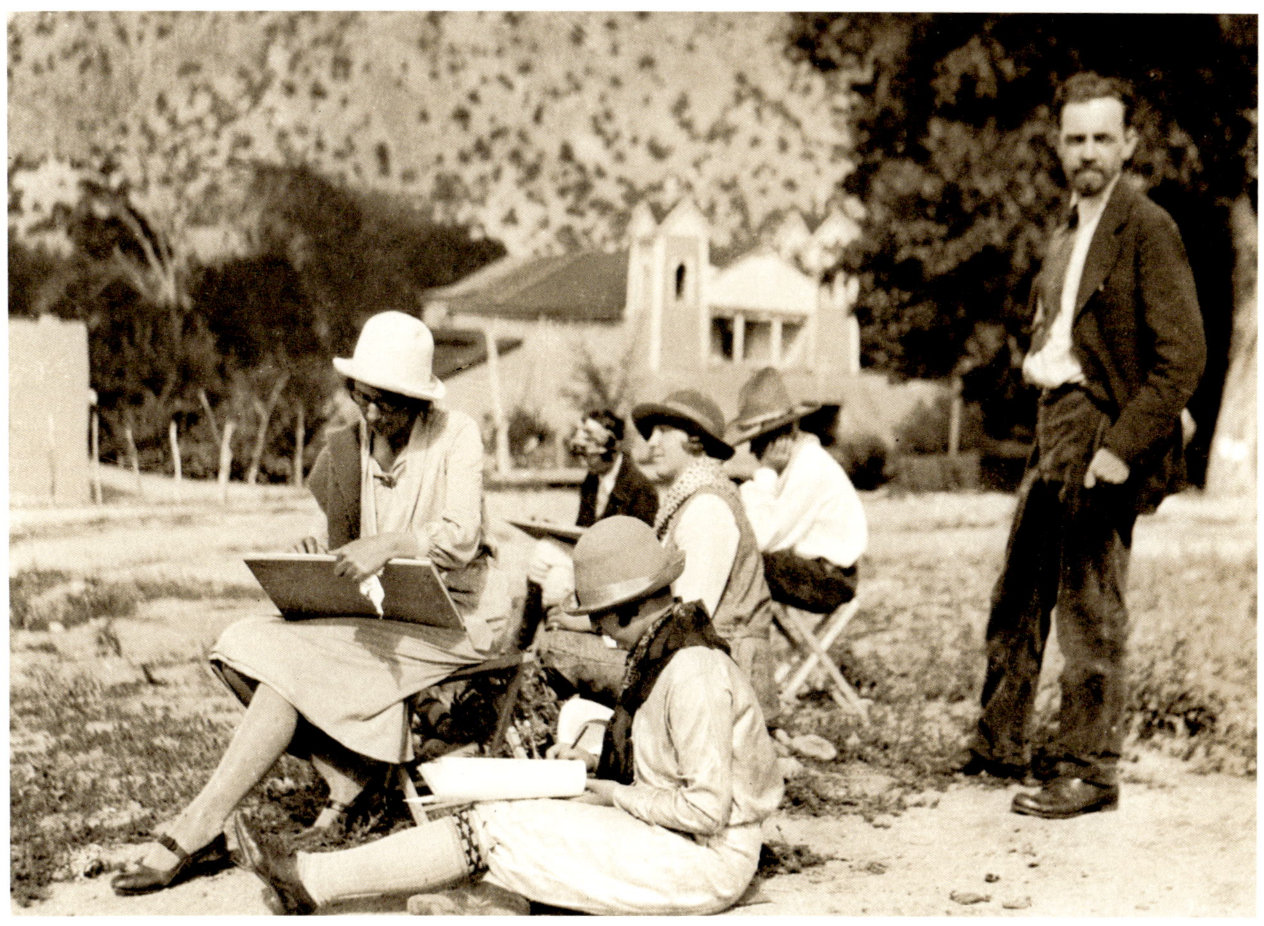

Fig. 4. Raymond Jonson, owner of Atalaya Art School, on field trip with his students to Santuario de Chimayo, Chimayo, New Mexico, c. 1926.

ists and civic leaders. The latter group included writer Mary Austin, poet Witter Bynner, arts patron Amelia Elizabeth White, and Senator Bronson Cutting. Artist supporters were Dasburg, Cassidy, and Jonson (whose Atalaya Art School had closed the previous season). The Santa Fe Art School had completed two successful summers when Kay-Scott was persuaded to accept the directorship of the Denver Art Museum. His new employer agreed, however, to allow Kay-Scott to return for summer classes in Santa Fe, leaving the remainder of the school's program, by now expanded to year-round offer-ings, in the hands of a staff supervised by Cassidy. Though Santa Feans may have resented this second defection to Denver, the result was positive for both cities. Within a few years the Chappell Art School revived its summer program in Santa Fe, pooling its resources in the 1930s with those of the Santa Fe Art School.

Other schools flourished briefly from time to time. The Arsuna School of Art, for example, opened its doors in 1937 at Casa Querida, Mary Austin's residence at 439 Camino del Monte Sol. This spacious adobe, constructed in 1925, now houses the Gerald

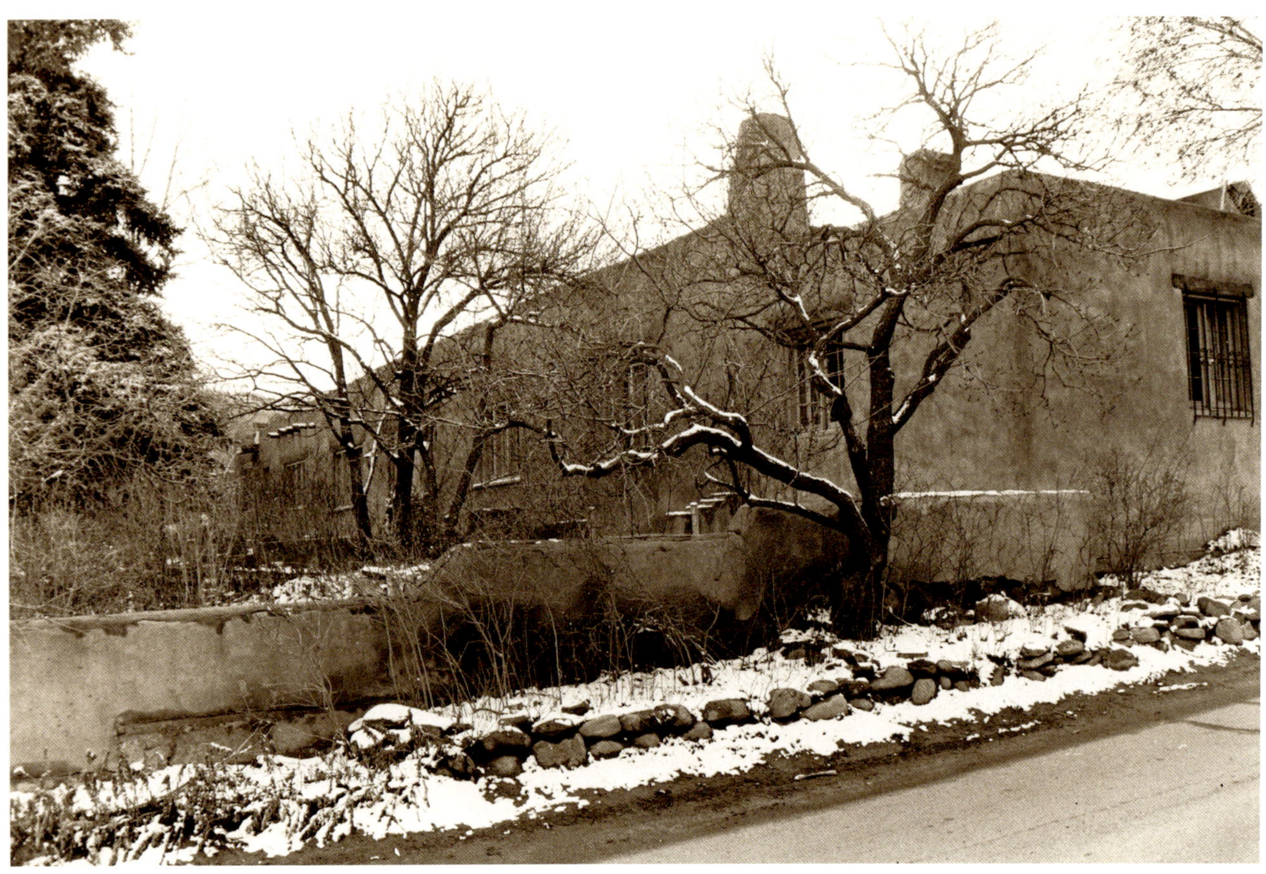

Fig. 5. Casa Querida, home of Mary Austin, built 1924, currently the Gerald Peters Gallery, Santa Fe, New Mexico.

Peters Gallery (fig. 5). The Arsuna School advertised courses in "painting; drawing; modeling and crafts; music; short story and feature writing."[20] Among its instructors were Jonson and Morang.

While art schools offered jobs to some Santa Fe painters, printmaking also provided opportunities to make a livelihood. Baumann, an accomplished color wood-block printer, taught printmaking to many younger artists over the years. Henry Balink and Baumann's longtime friend Nordfeldt were skilled printmakers as well as painters. Balink's etchings of Indian subjects complemented his oil portraits, and Nordfeldt's etchings of his Hispanic neighbors became an important part of

his New Mexico oeuvre. Shuster and Nash honed their printmaking skills with Sloan and Nordfeldt. Rites of the Penitentes, which fascinated both Nordfeldt and Nash, were the subject of Nash's lithograph *Penitentes* (fig. 6). In etching and especially in lithography, Randall Davey found ways to expand the fleeting effects he created and the velvety dark tones he used with such skill. Later, Lloyd Moylan and Cady Wells found printmaking a rewarding artistic activity, as did Andrew Dasburg.

The museum played an important part in Santa Fe printmaking activities, as it did in so many other areas. It housed the first etching press brought to the area. Set up in the

20

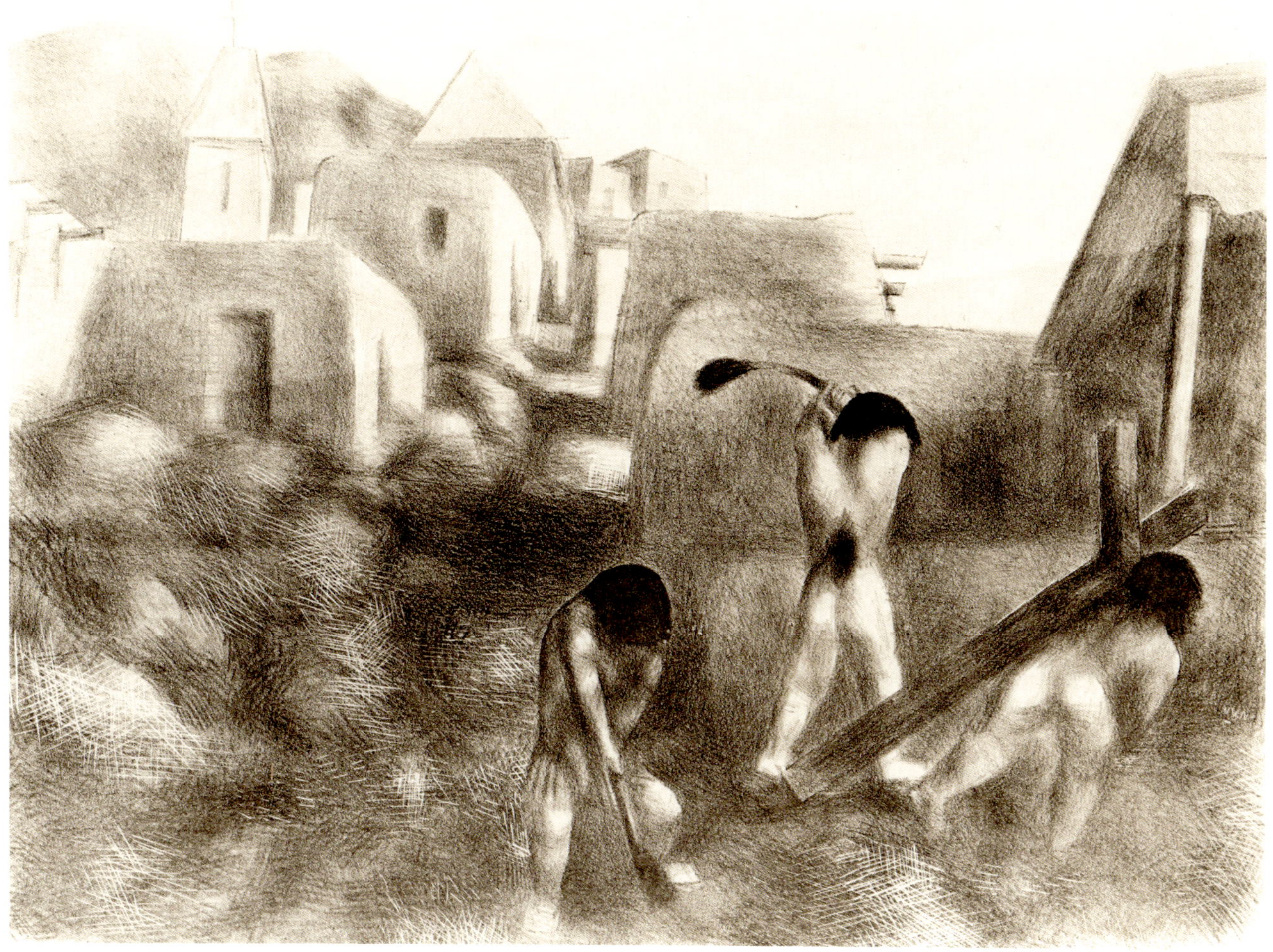

Fig. 6. Willard Nash, *Penitentes,* lithograph, 11½ × 15 in.

museum basement, it offered many artists the opportunity to explore the subtleties of black and white and to create multiples of their images. Printmaking naturally led to print exhibitions, and lower print prices created sales for the artists even when painting sales were few. Nordfeldt shared his print-making expertise as early as 1919, when he addressed a gathering at the Santa Fe Print Shop, a gallery in which Alice Corbin Henderson had part interest. This small shop exhibited the work of local printmakers but also showed work in other media. Hartley, for example, was invited to show his New Mexico pastels in the shop's opening exhibit. In May 1919 the gallery displayed watercolors and drawings by Charles Demuth and Charles Sheeler, two of the bright young stars in the New York art world. A second print gallery, the Print Room, operated in Sena Plaza in the early 1930s. Its existence testified to the continued interest in print-making in Santa Fe.

Along with these specialized print galleries, commercial exhibition space slowly became more plentiful. Retail shops and the First National Bank offered alternative space to artists. In the summer of 1923, for example, Fremont Ellis showed pastels at what was called the Mariposa Shop. The Pioneer Art Gallery and Tea Room operated on East Palace Avenue in the late twenties. The names of various small galleries appear in press accounts from the twenties and thirties; some, such as that operated by Jane Baumann in Sena Plaza exclusively to retail her husband's works, were efforts to bypass the gallery middleman. She eventually moved the outlet to their home. Another natural way to place art in the path of visitors was to locate a gallery in a hotel: La Fonda, a Fred Harvey hotel filled with Hispanic-inspired interior decorations, was a favorite gathering and exhibition space for artists in the 1930s.

In 1938 the Santa Fe Gallery opened in Sena Plaza. Devoted primarily to the work of southwestern artists, it boasted prices ranging from fifty cents for "an attractive etching" to a thousand dollars for "an important oil."[21] Featured, too, at the Santa Fe Gallery were items as diverse as Julian Martinez's San Ildefonso pottery, Native American painting, and—a somewhat incongruous addition—"original paintings on celluloid by Walt Disney: the actual paintings from which the famous movies have been made."[22]

The diverse offerings of Santa Fe's art museum and its private galleries suggest a growing audience for old and new art forms in the Southwest in the 1920s and 1930s. Outside museums and galleries, visitors had been able to see murals by New Mexico artists for years. Ancient Indian wall paintings, such as those discovered at the Pottery Mound and Kuaua sites in New Mexico, seem a model of large-scale painting for late-nineteenth and early twentieth-century artists. The activity of Santa Fe artists was visible as early as 1915, when San Diego hosted the Panama-California Exposition. The exposition celebrated nothing less than the "Progress of Man and his achievements in the completion of the Panama Canal."[23] Edgar Hewett, who served as director of exhibits, hired Santa Feans Carlos Vierra and Gerald Cassidy to paint murals for five rooms dedicated to the Science of Man exhibit in the California Building. The two artists, struggling to make a living, were grateful for the work. Cassidy fared particularly well, receiving a gold medal for his work, which survives today in Balboa Park, where the exposition took place.

When the Santa Fe Fine Arts Museum, a replica of New Mexico's pueblo-inspired building at the San Diego Exposition, opened in 1917, its chief patron, Frank Springer, also wanted murals. Springer commissioned a young Utah-born artist, Donald Beauregard, to provide an ambitious mural series based on the life of St. Francis for the auditorium. Upon Beauregard's untimely death, Vierra and Kenneth Chapman finished the work, which remains today.

Mural paintings occupied many other Santa Fe artists in subsequent years. Willard Nash first visited New Mexico in 1920 to gather visual material for a Detroit mural. Over the years, a number of businesses have decorated their walls with paintings by Santa Feans, such as Shuster's Fiesta scenes at El Nido Restaurant, still thriving in Tesuque, just north of Santa Fe. And, in 1937, Davey was hired, with Bakos assisting, to paint murals at the Will Rogers Shrine in Colorado Springs.

Wall paintings in Texas and New Mexico fascinated Russel Vernon Hunter before he ever completed a mural himself. Like Stuart Davis, he especially enjoyed the monumental advertisements that sometimes covered the entire side of a building. Hunter's American Mural series, including *Old Mesilla* and *Texico, New Mexico,* are easel paintings that capture the scale and humor of 1930s' advertising art (pls. 26 and 27).

But it was the Public Works of Art Project, the Treasury Relief Art Project, and the Works Progress Administration (WPA) programs that truly enriched the interiors of New Mexican architecture. Four men between 1933 and 1943 administered federally sponsored arts programs in New Mexico: Jesse Nusbaum, an anthropologist and protégé of Hewett's who had assisted in the building of the Fine Arts Museum, and artists Gustave Baumann, Emil Bisttram, and Russel Vernon Hunter. Hunter, who became director of the Works Progress Administration in mid-1933, served the longest term, supervising completion of art works by some fifty-one New Mexico artists. Many Santa Feans participated in the programs, including Van Soelen, Bakos, Shuster, Moylan, Ellis, Henderson, Jonson, Nash, Cassidy, Nordfeldt, Parsons, and Olive Rush. Striking examples of 1930s' murals still exist throughout the state, such as Cassidy's in the Santa Fe Post Office, Henderson's in the Federal Court House, Santa Fe, and Lloyd Moylan's frescoes done in 1938 in the Administration Building, New Mexico Highlands University, Las Vegas.

In New Mexico, as elsewhere, government support for the arts affected artistic life. In Santa Fe, no one style reigned supreme, and tradition and innovation could be found in different proportions. But it was tradition that received a boost from the federal arts projects. Baumann, for example, welcomed the program's generally conservative stylistic bias, seeing it as a corrective to the brand of hyperrefined "artiness" of the community in the 1920s. Modernism, to these conservatives, divided artists from their audience, creating a cultural gap between the initiated artist and the uninitiated public. Under federal patronage, themes and styles merged briefly into an acceptable, understandable artistic whole.

A famous example of the collision of "progress" with the past occurred in 1926 when a group of Federated Women's Clubs proposed that a Chautauqua, a summer culture colony popular in the East, be started in Santa Fe. It would draw some 3,000 extra visitors to the town each year: not just ordinary tourists, its proponents argued, but well-educated, affluent Texans whose dollars and refinement would doubly enrich the area. Not so, snorted opponents! Mary Austin, deploring "these yearners" after culture, marshalled the artists and writers of the town to oppose the Chautauqua, while Hewett, the Chamber of Commerce, and the political Old Guard supported it. Hot arguments recorded in the press exposed the art community's cultural elitism. The fracas reached the pages of the New York *World,* in which Albuquerque writer Kyle Crichton, identified as a man of scrupulous impartiality, called it "The great battle of Santa Fe . . . a deadly combat between two philosophies, between the Philistine and the Artist, between Progress and Atmosphere." [24]

Though the Chautauqua proposal was defeated by the Austin, Bynner, Sloan, Old Santa Fe Association forces, unanswered questions remained. The once-somnolent village must inevitably grow and change; this everyone knew. But how would an expanded population affect the artistic environment and, more specifically, the artists' favorite subjects? What would happen, for example, to the Indians of the area—living links to America's aboriginal past? It was their long-standing harmonious connection with the land that inspired so many artists. Long a subject of interest to anthropologists, the Indian had been seen by generations of world-weary easterners as "noble savages," whose art and life were perfectly integrated. The Indian was, after all, America's first artist. And, threatened by Hispanic and Anglo encroachment, his predicted disappearance in the face of "progress" prompted much interest in him as a subject for painters. Some artists, like Henry Balink, continued a documentary tradition established in the nineteenth century by artists such as George Catlin and Karl Bodmer. Like his predecessors, Balink intended to portray accurately members of many tribes. But Balink's *The Drummer* is a more generalized view of the Indian. Minimizing ethnological details, he has instead created a careful orchestration of textures: facial skin is subtly contrasted with the drum head and his leather clothing (pl. 5). Similar yet more romantic, Julius Rolshoven in *Navajo Maiden* emphasizes warm skin tones and lushly colored fabrics to create an inviting yet demure portrait. This painting, which includes in the background another colorful painting by Rolshoven, is a clear example of this artist's remarkable brushwork (pl. 47).

Warm tonalities predominate in Warren Rollins's painting, *The Navajo,* where a graceful blending of curves and angles enhances the watchful, intent expression of the sitter (pl. 45).

Similar in subject but much freer in handling is Gerald Cassidy's *Big Mike the Apache:* the aging warrior remains a noble exemplar of his tribe (pl. 10). The focused, suspicious gaze of Henri's *Portrait of an Indian* seems to ask us, the viewers, to explain our presence (pl. 24). Here Henri balances warm and cool tones with bold patterning and bravura brushwork to ignite this compelling painting. In contrast to Henri's painting, we know little of the sitter's mood in Shuster's *The Pottery Maker* (pl. 48). Patiently decorating her work, the Pueblo woman is defined by what she does—by the work of her hands.

If individual Indians provided great breadth of artistic interpretation, so, too, did Indians in daily activity or ceremonial gatherings. Henry Balink's *On the Old Santa Fe Trail,* enlivened by an Impressionist-inspired palette, sets a traveling Indian family against the snowcapped grandeur of the New Mexico mountains (pl. 3). A closely allied subject is presented in Cassidy's *Evening Meal, Navajo Land,* in which more detail is introduced into the high-desert landscape—horses, wagon, and sculptured rock formations all sharing a solidity of form (pl. 11). Rollins's *The Thrall of the Past/Zuni Pueblo* suggests the beauty inherent in simple daily tasks performed with dignity (pl. 46).

The southwestern Indian shown within the context of a ceremonial or dance loses individuality captured by the portraitist but gains collective identity. The needs of individuals in Pueblo culture are secondary to

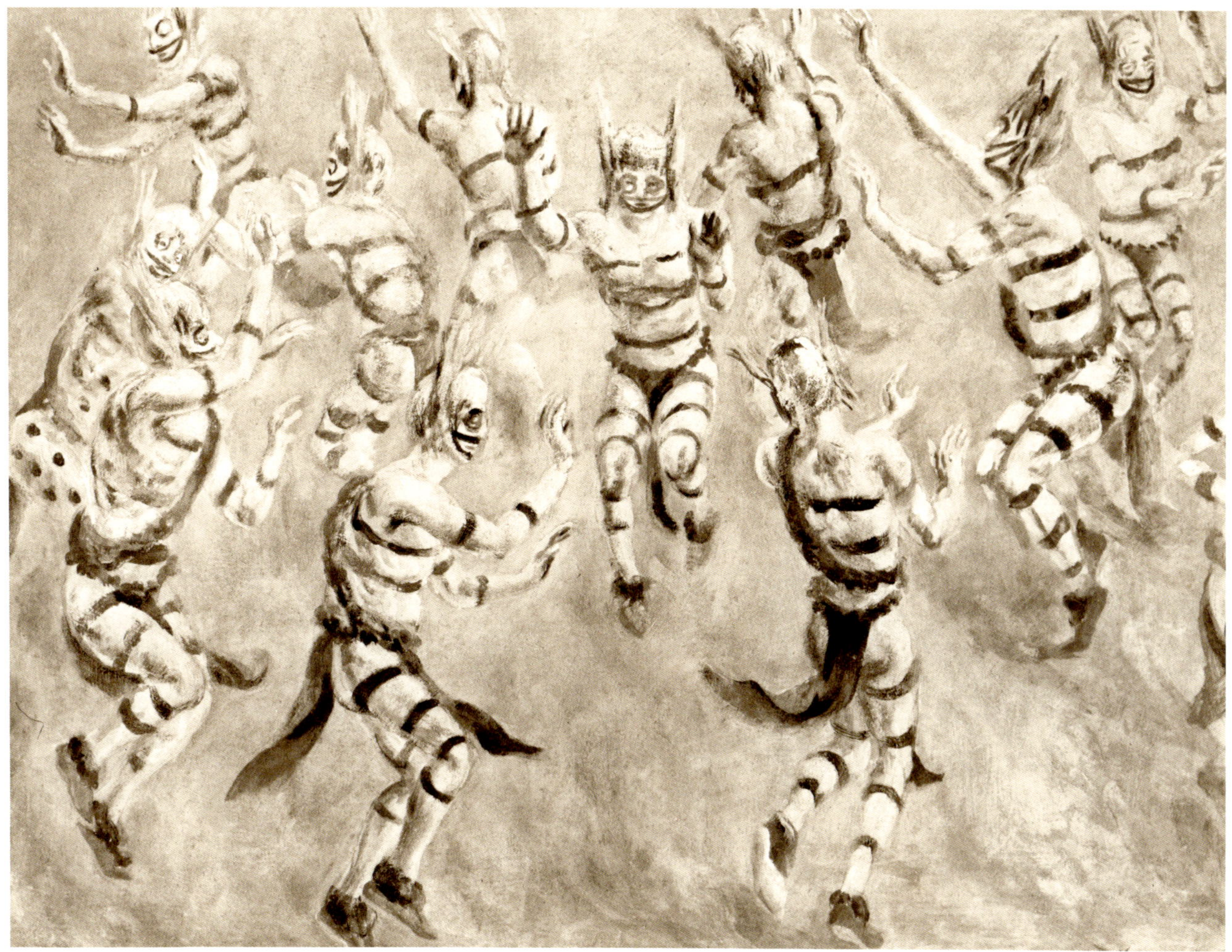

Fig. 7. John Sloan, *Koshare in the Dust,* 1930, tempera with oil-varnish glazes on panel, 19¾ × 25¾ in.

the goals of the group; in turn, the group is guided by traditions intended to maintain harmony with nature through ceremony. Artists suggest their fascination with this communal characteristic of Pueblo life by uniting figure with figure and figure with earth in rhythmic patterns of shape, color, and line. This unifying stylization is intended ultimately to suggest the spiritual wholeness of Pueblo Indian life. B. J. O. Nordfeldt creates in *Indian Dance (Foot Race — San Juan)* a sense of energy and movement that not only binds the dancers to each other but to the

landscape (pl. 38). Drawing on structural lessons found in the work of Cézanne, Nordfeldt's patchy brushwork punctuates the composition like drumbeats. More solemn and measured are the rhythmic intervals within Balink's *Chief Dance* (pl. 4). Here the anonymity of the dancers, like that of the rooftop spectators, underscores the collective spirit of the Pueblos.

Rhythm, too, is suggested in William Penhallow Henderson's *Before the Shrine, San Ildefonso,* where solid thud-thuds of moccasined feet find a visual analogue in the solid forms of the dancers (pl. 23). Henderson's vivid color heightens the richness of the scene. The rhythm of colored shapes and curvilinear forms in *Corn Dance* and *Koshare in the Dust* by Gina Knee and John Sloan, respectively, suggests artistic sensibilities impatient with detail, intent on sensations expressed through movement (pl. 33 and fig. 7). Russel Vernon Hunter isolated two dancers from a crowd of onlookers in *Native Dancers* (pl. 28). Though we confront them closely, the male and female screen their thoughts from us. Hunter's strong color suits the boldly drawn contours of their bodies.

The observers of the dances are the subject of Lloyd Moylan's *Indian Ceremonial* (pl. 35). These Navajos, whom Moylan has seen as a colorful arrangement of form and pattern subsumed within the larger spectacle of the dance, suggest again the cultural significance of the ceremonial to the Indian way of life.

As artists worked to record the changing culture of the Native Americans, they also observed the history and character of the region's Hispanic population. The striking physical features of the Hispanics and their proud cultural heritage, born of three hundred years in the Santa Fe area, attracted many painters. Fremont Ellis's imposing *El Caballero,* who poses in his boldly striped Navajo chief's blanket against warm adobe walls, is a graceful gesture to the past painted by a respectful artist (pl. 19). Equally appreciative of his Hispanic neighbors was Nordfeldt, whose *Man with Brown Suspenders* has an ageless solidity about it. Hat in his lap, the subject waits — for his portrait? for the years to pass? for what unforeseeable changes? (pl. 39).

A livelier portrayal of an Hispanic subject comes from the brush of Homer Boss, whose *Nina* gives the viewer a forthright gaze (pl. 8). Richly patterned fabrics recalling a tradition of weaving practiced for centuries by Indians and Hispanics in the Southwest contrasts with the sitter's youth. Paul Burlin, who carefully avoided sentimental conventions in his paintings of New Mexico Indians, likewise shunned clichés in his Hispanic subjects, as in *Girl with Flower* (pl. 9).

His Hispanic and Indian neighbors, then, gave the Santa Fe artist insight into a past that was being eroded yearly by the influx of visitors and new residents. But what of the landscape itself? In a place where mere looking often became an act of devotion, what effects would a burgeoning population bring? In New Mexico the landscape had always played the starring role in defining the character of the place. Unlike the green predictabilities of the East, New Mexico had a raw, unfinished quality to its topography. Stepping off a westbound train, artists were confronted with an achingly bright light, a chorus of cacophonic color, and land forms described by Hartley and John Marin as "chaotic." All this must have seemed an overt attack on refined, academy-trained sensibilities. Who could — or should — inhabit this glorious, elusive landscape? Could one possess it by painting it? Or was it best recorded briefly by artists who then slipped quietly away, leaving it to the birds overhead?

Of those whose brushes stalked the pristine wildness, Homer Boss takes the land on its own, outspoken terms in *Red Clay Formation* (pl. 7). Awestruck, too, by the power of nature's forms was John Sloan, whose *Little Ranch House* seems to suggest the futility of

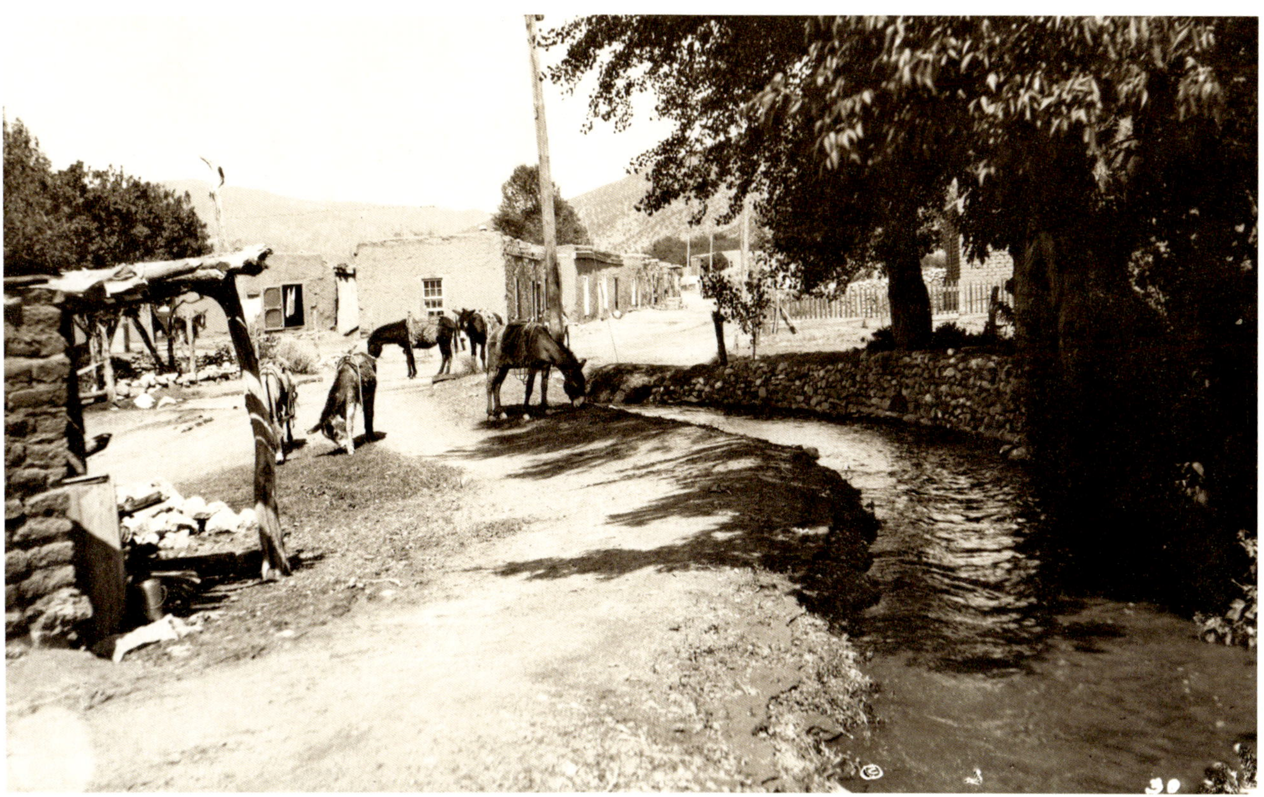

Fig. 8. Burros at Acequia Madre, Santa Fe, New Mexico, c. 1915.

human intervention in such a place (pl. 51). Raymond Jonson's *Arroyo, Santa Fe Sketch* depicts the raw power of nature in the Southwest, where flash floods can bring a dry arroyo to surging life (pl. 32). Quite different is the benign face of nature revealed in Sheldon Parsons' *Pojoaque, New Mexico,* in which water flows gently through an acequia, or canal (pl. 43). Delicate patterns in the tree branches are born again along the water's edge, as if to suggest the regenerative power of water in the dry Southwest. The importance of water to New Mexico communities is shown by homes built close to the acequia, the source of all life (fig. 8).

John Sloan's *Picnic in the Rio Grande Canyon* also catches flowing water in a beneficent mood (fig. 9). The artist began the painting as a closely observed record of a specific place but changed it substantially as work continued in the studio. "The design became less naturalistic," wrote Sloan. "I started to feel my way to a more abstract emphasis by redrawing one of the trees and working out a more tactile handling of the foliage. This led to changes elsewhere, experiments in color and value."[25]

The land inevitably gave way to man's need to thrive and provide food and shelter. Theodore Van Soelen's *Grazing Cattle* portrays those early western settlers who first tamed the range (pl. 52). Herded by three cowboys, the white-faced cattle move slowly among the sage and juniper, as violet-hued shadows enter the soft red cliffs beyond. Jonson, too, saw nature transformed by man's

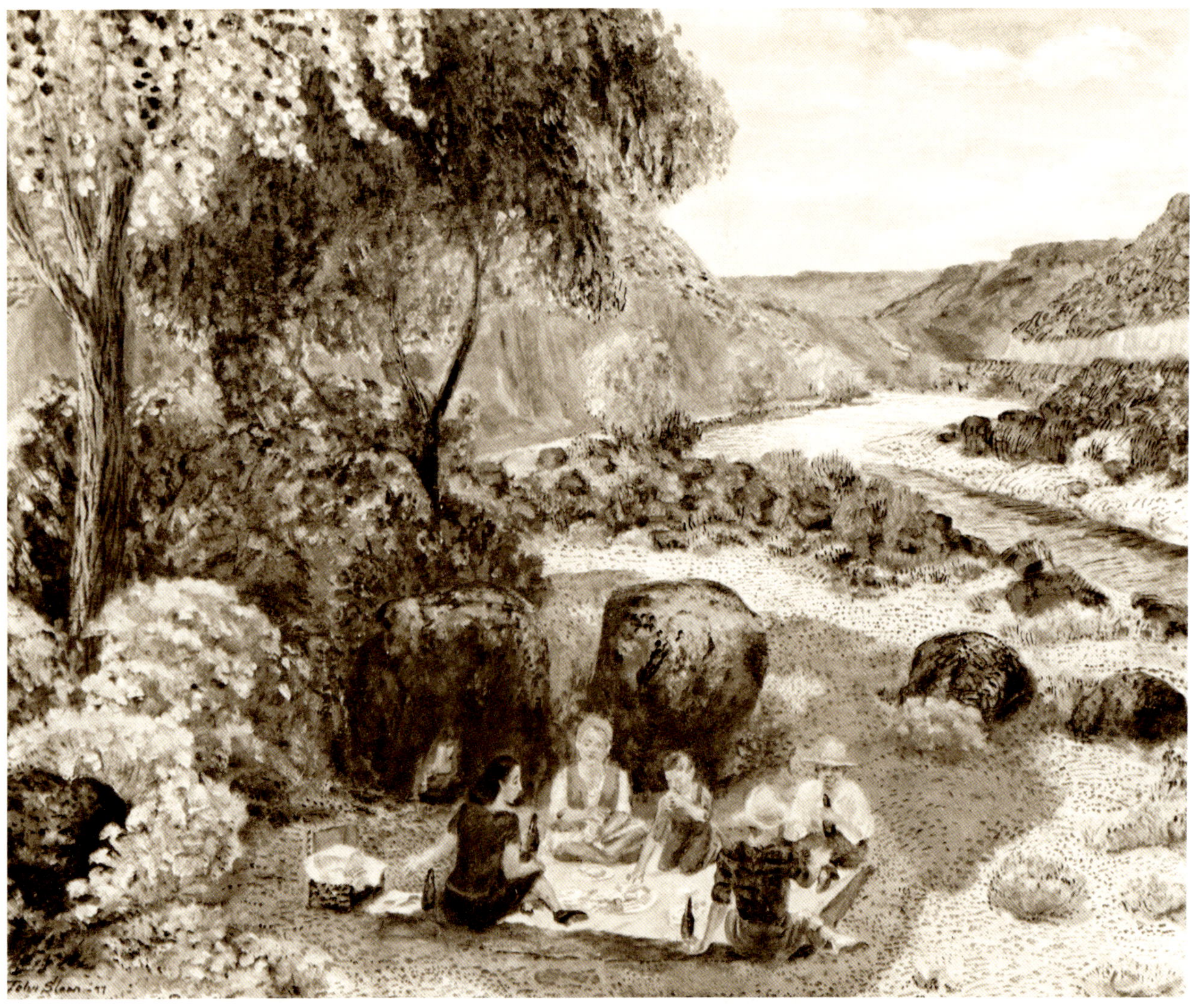

Fig. 9. John Sloan, *Picnic in the Rio Grande Canyon,* 1938, tempera with oil-varnish glazes on panel, 19¾ × 23¾ in.

need to civilize. In *Blue Roofs* and *Spanish Quarters,* the blocky shapes of adobes claim the solidity of the earth itself, while in the slightly later *Santa Fe Placita* Jonson's freer distortions lend a fragile, folded-paper quality to the buildings (pls. 30, 31, and 29).

Others, as well, painted New Mexico as it yielded to settlement. Cyrus Baldridge domesticates New Mexico in *Field,* the land he depicts not vast and irrational but dominated by ordered furrows (pl. 2). Andrew Dasburg,

too, imposed order on the New Mexico desert, as he does in *Taos Scene,* a checkerboard pattern of plowed fields, and in *October Landscape,* a town of cubes caught within a shallow, shifting cubist space (pls. 13 and 14). Similarly, Jozef Bakos juxtaposed the angularities of buildings against a rugged terrain, as in *Tularoja Peak, Santa Fe, New Mexico* (pl. 1).

Following Dasburg's lead, Cady Wells also found angle and curve in New Mexico's topography. Sometimes he emphasized chaos, as in *Mountain Peak near Abiquiu;* sometimes flowing calligraphic sweeps, as in *Black Mesa* (pls. 56 and 55).

Time within the New Mexico landscape can be charted in both geological and spiritual terms. Before it was ever painted, the land marked time in the stirrings of Mother Earth and Father Sky. Sacred in its rarified juxtapositions of the eternal and the ephemeral, the land had no need of tight chronologies. Fortunately, many artists who came to New Mexico were genuinely sensitive to its antiquity, even when they thought in shorter time increments. Lloyd Moylan's *Adobe Church,* with its jumble of crosses in the *camposanto,* suggests on one hand the enduring qualities of the church as a building and as an institution and on the other the ephemerality of human life (pl. 36).

Always, the passage of time is marked by the changing seasons. Some New Mexico artists became deservedly famous for their portrayals of the changing color of foliage. Ellis's sun-dappled *Road Through Cottonwoods* hints at cooler days to come (pl. 20). Golden cottonwoods, like autumn sunshine, lend warmth to Sheldon Parsons' *Near San Ildefonso, New Mexico* and Shuster's *Cottonwoods, Tesuque* (pls. 41 and 50).

Artists portrayed the winter season less frequently, yet when they did the results were often striking. Snow softly blanketing adobe walls and roofs takes on a warm tonality in Parsons' *February in Alcalde,* while in Davey's *Upper Canyon Road* the snow contrasts with the still-colorful roadside vegetation (pls. 42 and 15). In Vierra's *Northern New Mexico in Winter,* a fast-approaching winter storm warns of more snow for the al-

ready blanketed hills (pl. 54). But winter changes cannot extinguish the light and color of the New Mexico landscape.

The scores of artists who wandered the Santa Fe environs on horseback or bounced in touring cars over bone-jarring roads gradually enjoyed easier access to painting sites. But if roads and trails improved, the recalcitrance of the landscape did not. Each succeeding generation, lured by warm adobe walls, the blue shadows of tenacious juniper against the snow, and puffy clouds extruded into a canopy of blue, had to balance New Mexico's exquisite realities against the difficulties of capturing them on canvas. For many artists the initial shock of the landscape—its earth and sky locked in uneasy combat for visual dominance—was too much of a good thing. They longed for a place where light could be managed, where human scale determined internal relationships among painted forms. Some found it within walled gardens or flower-bordered lanes, where nature seemed arrayed in more human proportions. In his color wood-block prints, Baumann explored this quiet, meditative aspect of nature much as he did in such paintings as *A Burst of Spring* (pl. 6). Van Soelen, too, often made peace with nature, as when he painted such familiar Santa Fe landmarks as the home of Witter Bynner, which he titled *The Poet's House* (pl. 53).

Still other Santa Fe painters found manageable light and scale within the concrete reality of a table top. Not that still-life painting must be seen as a retreat from the New Mexico landscape; for many painters a finite, rearrangeable space offers infinite creative challenge. But in a still life the artist, not nature, sets up formal problems to be solved.

For Randall Davey, the lusciousness of paint was its own excuse for being. In *Flowers on a Marble Table* the dense mass of color sets off the pristine whiteness of a casually placed note (pl. 18). Spikier flower forms and complementary colors set up their own rhythms within *Still Life—Flowers in a Vase* (pl. 17). Andrew Dasburg imposed on his still-life subjects some of the same formal rigor as he did on his landscapes. His *Still Life (Poppies)* embraces an angular Cézanne-Cubist vision in the canted table top and patchy color, while allowing the curved poppy stems their own graceful arabesque (pl. 12). Nordfeldt's *Roses and Canvas* is art about art (frontispiece). A shallow, shifting space is created by the nearly monochromatic arrangement of canvas and frames, while three garden roses spill casually from an enameled pitcher: nature at the service of the artist's vision.

Marsden Hartley painted nature with a brooding intensity. The twisting branches of his *Fig Tree,* like grasping tentacles, are alive and menacing (pl. 22). Another artist might have revealed in neat slices the lusciousness of a melon's flesh; painted by Hartley, however, a gaping jagged hole in *Cantaloupe* speaks of a savage attack by an unseen knife (pl. 21). There is an almost physical sense of pain here, the counterpart on canvas of Hartley's own psychic pain. As always, Hartley's dramatic and personal view of nature is expressed by powerfully painted forms. Russel Vernon Hunter employed the opposite end of the emotional spectrum in *Trading Post, Dallas* (pl. 25). Here, a sense of whimsy invades the store window, where a clutter of souvenirs intrigues the eye and provides a rush of recognition.

Santa Fe's haphazardly cultivated artistic character was and is at once its bane and its chief source of pride. From its beginnings, the town attracted painters of all artistic persuasions. Sophisticated East Coast avantgarde artists rubbed shoulders with those whose roots lay in the West. For both, the larger world intruded. Yet, as the mid-twentieth century approached and Los Alamos helped the world find new ways to extinguish its natural sources of life, even the atomic bomb could not efface the creative spirit of New Mexico. Artists have continued to refine what is distinctive and true in the local environment while avoiding the self-satisfied insularity that could have buried Santa Fe in its own picturesque legend. This exhibition, while not intended to present an exhaustive picture of painting in Santa Fe, can at least suggest the richness and diversity of that living heritage.

Sharyn Rohlfsen Udahll

Notes

1. "Santa Fe Sketches." In *Good Morning, America.* Copyright 1928, 1956 by Carl Sandburg. Reprinted by permission of Harcourt Brace Jovanovich, Inc.
2. Chauvenet, p. 140.
3. "New Mexico Fine Arts." *The Santa Fean.* 2 (September 1974), p. 27.
4. *El Palacio* 3, no. 4 (1916), p. 87. Later titles of these annual Fiesta shows were numbered as if they had begun in 1914.
5. Col. José D. Sena, Letter, *Santa Fe New Mexican.* 21 April 1915, p. 4.
6. Edgar L. Hewett. "Art Policy of Museum and School." *El Palacio* 10, no. 5 (1921), p. 2.
7. ———. "Art Policy." p. 3.
8. White (1983).
9. *El Palacio* 11, no. 12 (1921), p. 164.
10. *El Palacio* 14, no. 8 (1923), pp. 123–24.
11. *Ibid.*
12. *El Palacio* 13, no. 10 (1922), p. 132.
13. White (1986).
14. *El Palacio* 14, no. 8 (1923), p. 124.
15. Henry C. Balink, quoted in Jones, p. 96.
16. John Sloan, quoted in *The New York Times* article reprinted in *El Palacio* 12, no. 12 (1922), p. 170.
17. Randall Davey, quoted in Hoopes (1979), p. 49.
18. *El Palacio* 19, no. 4 (1925), p. 63.
19. *El Palacio* 24, nos. 20–21 (1928), p. 409.
20. Advertisement, Artist's and Writer's Edition, *Santa Fe New Mexican,* 26 June 1940, p. 34.
21. "Santa Fe Gallery," Artist's and Writer's Edition, p. 28.
22. *Ibid.*
23. Chauvenet, p. 105.
24. Kyle S. Crichton. "Philistine and Artist Clash in Battle of Santa Fe." New York *World,* 27 June 1926. Copy in files of Old Santa Fe Association, Santa Fe, New Mexico.
25. John Sloan, quoted in Kraft and Sloan, p. 68.

Plates

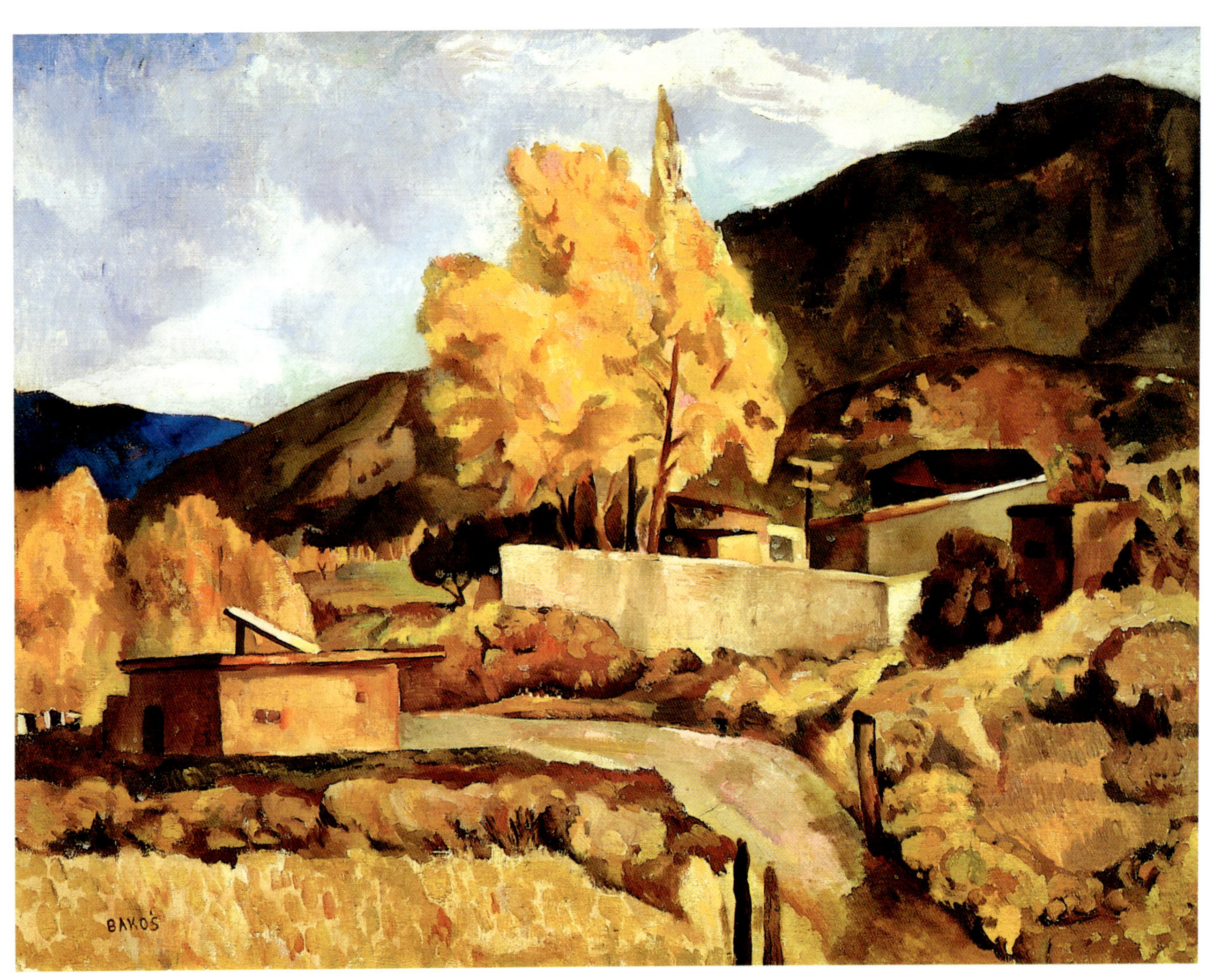

1. Jozef Bakos, *Tularoja Peak, Santa Fe, New Mexico,* oil on canvas, 25-1/2 × 32-1/4 in.

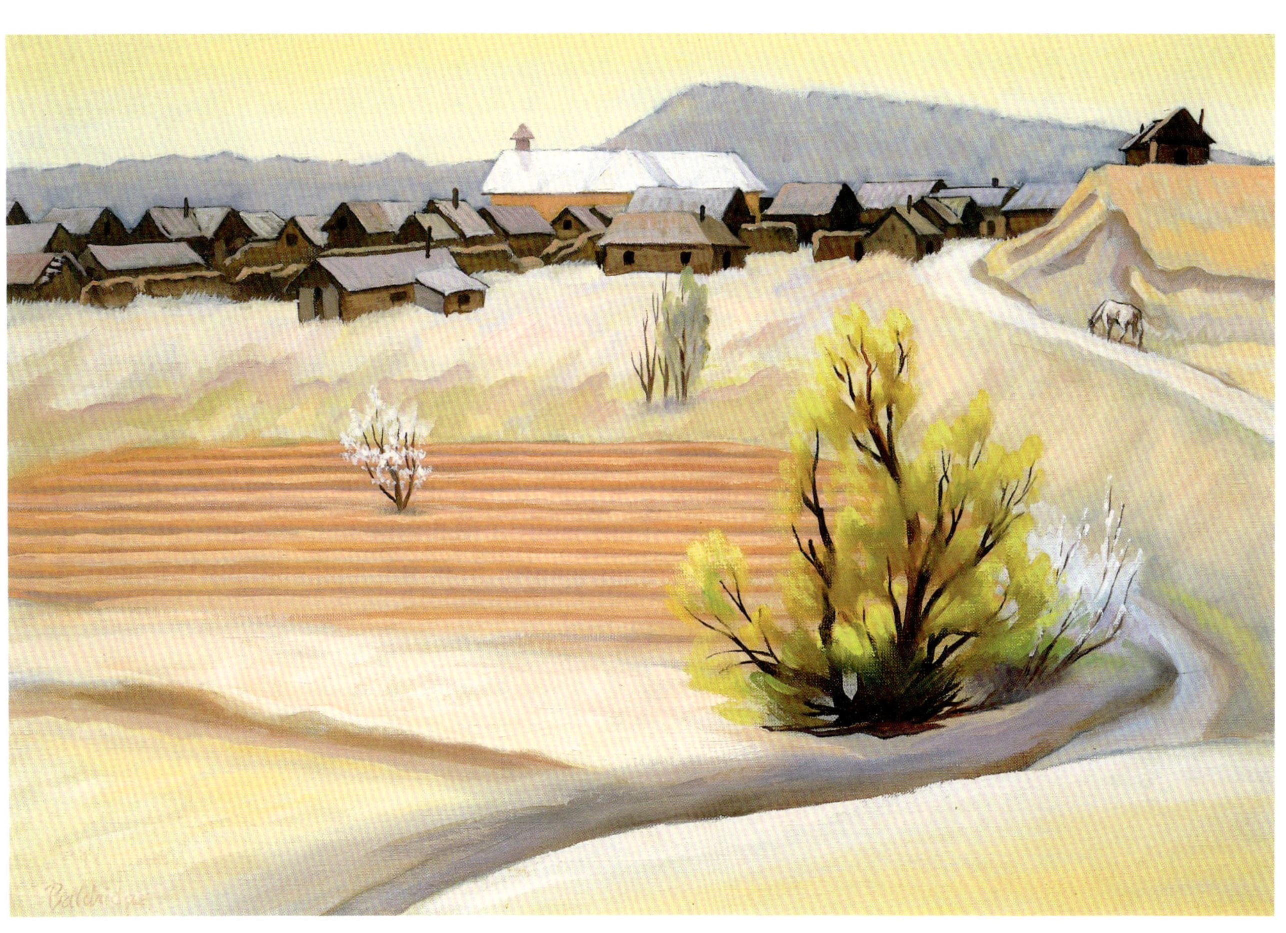

2. Cyrus Baldridge, *Field,* oil on canvas, 18 × 26 in.

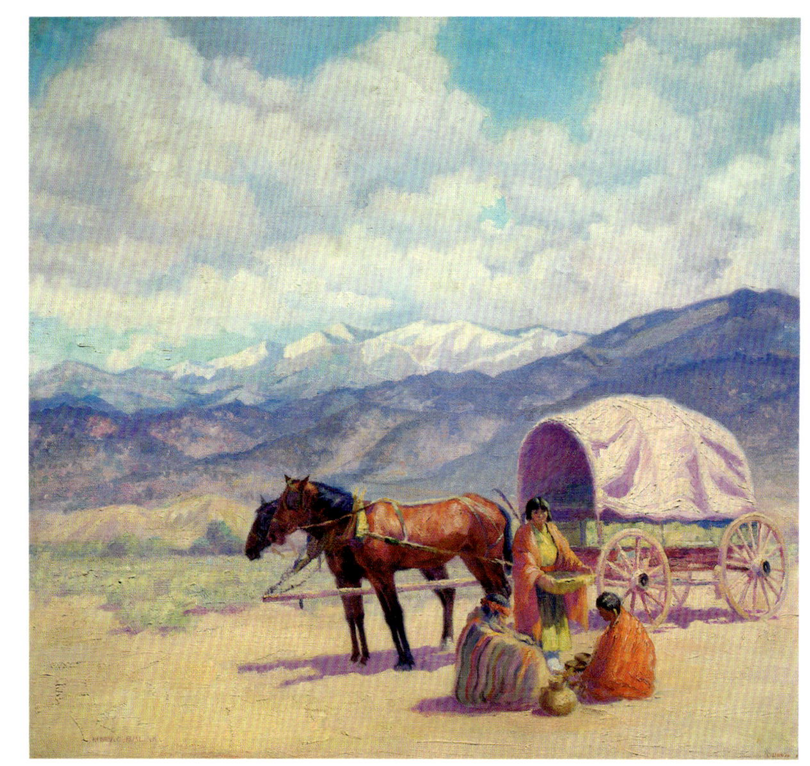

3. Henry Balink, *On the Old Santa Fe Trail,* oil on canvas, 35 × 37 in.

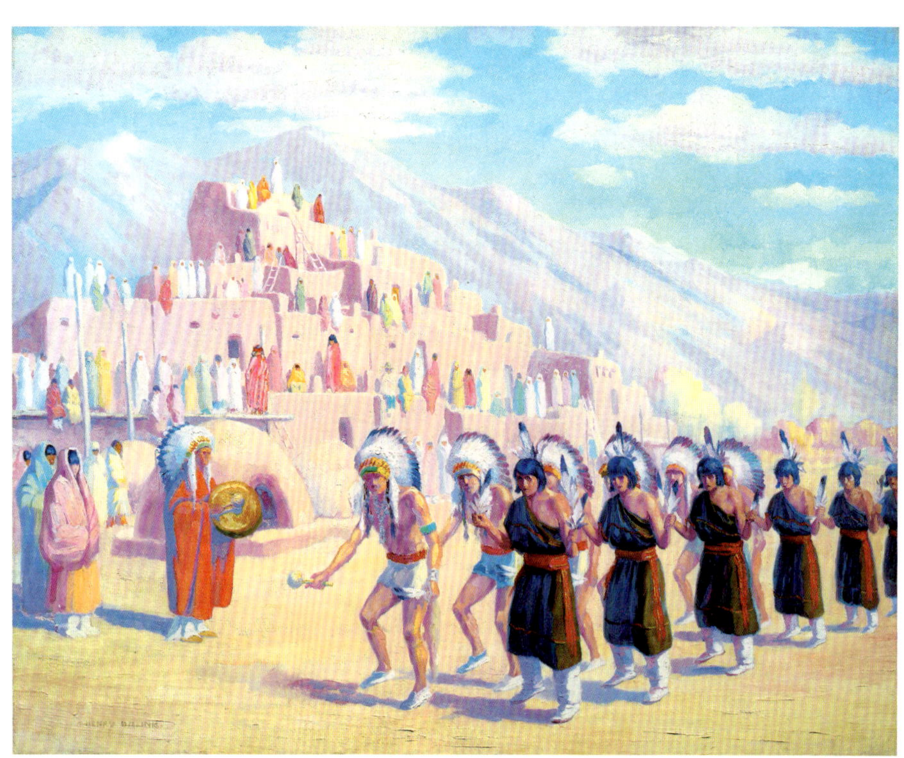

4. Henry Balink, *Chief Dance,* oil on canvas, 24 × 30 in.

36

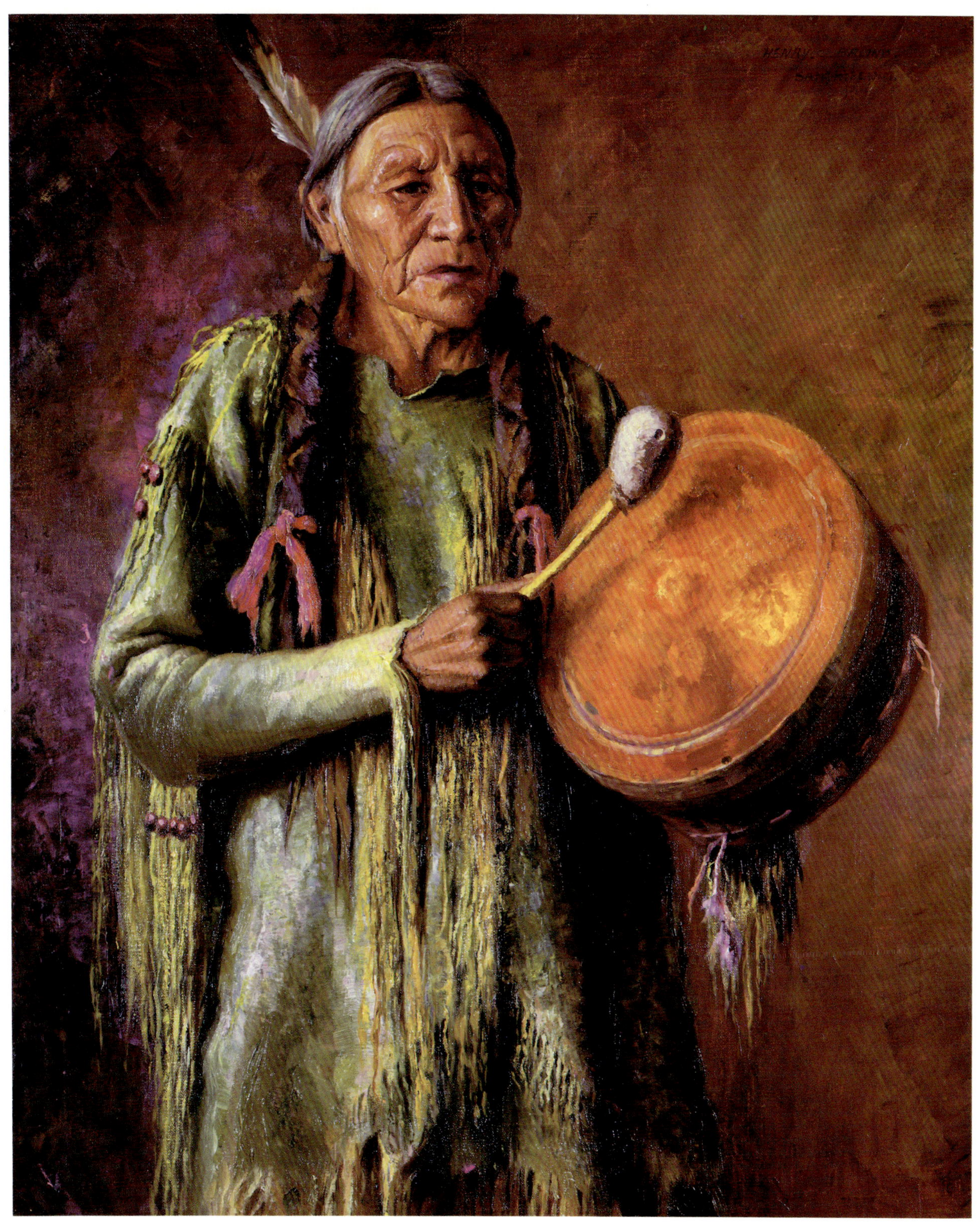

5. Henry Balink, *The Drummer,* oil on canvas, 30 × 25 in.

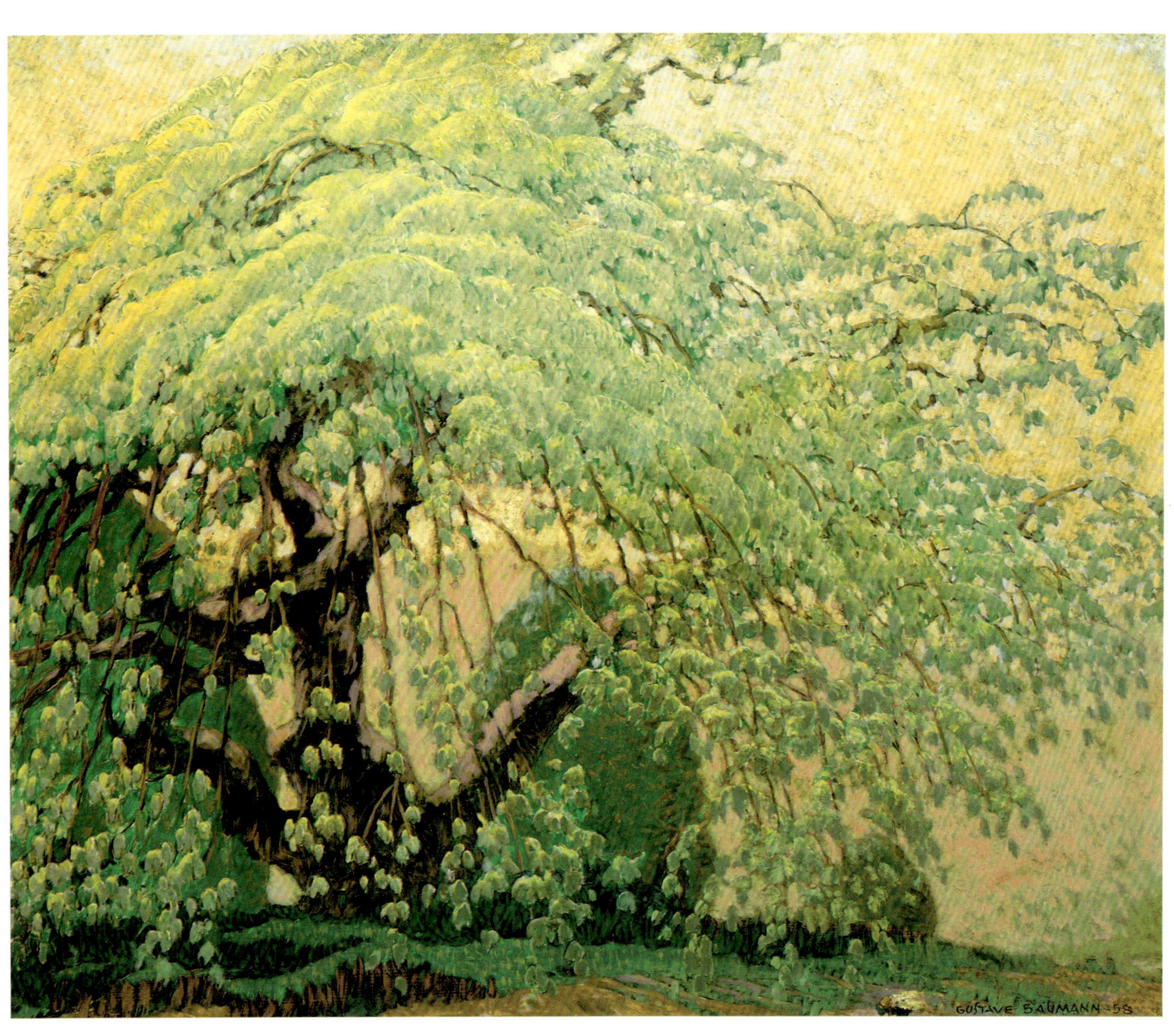

6. Gustave Baumann, *A Burst of Spring,* 1958, oil on canvas, 27 × 32 in.

38

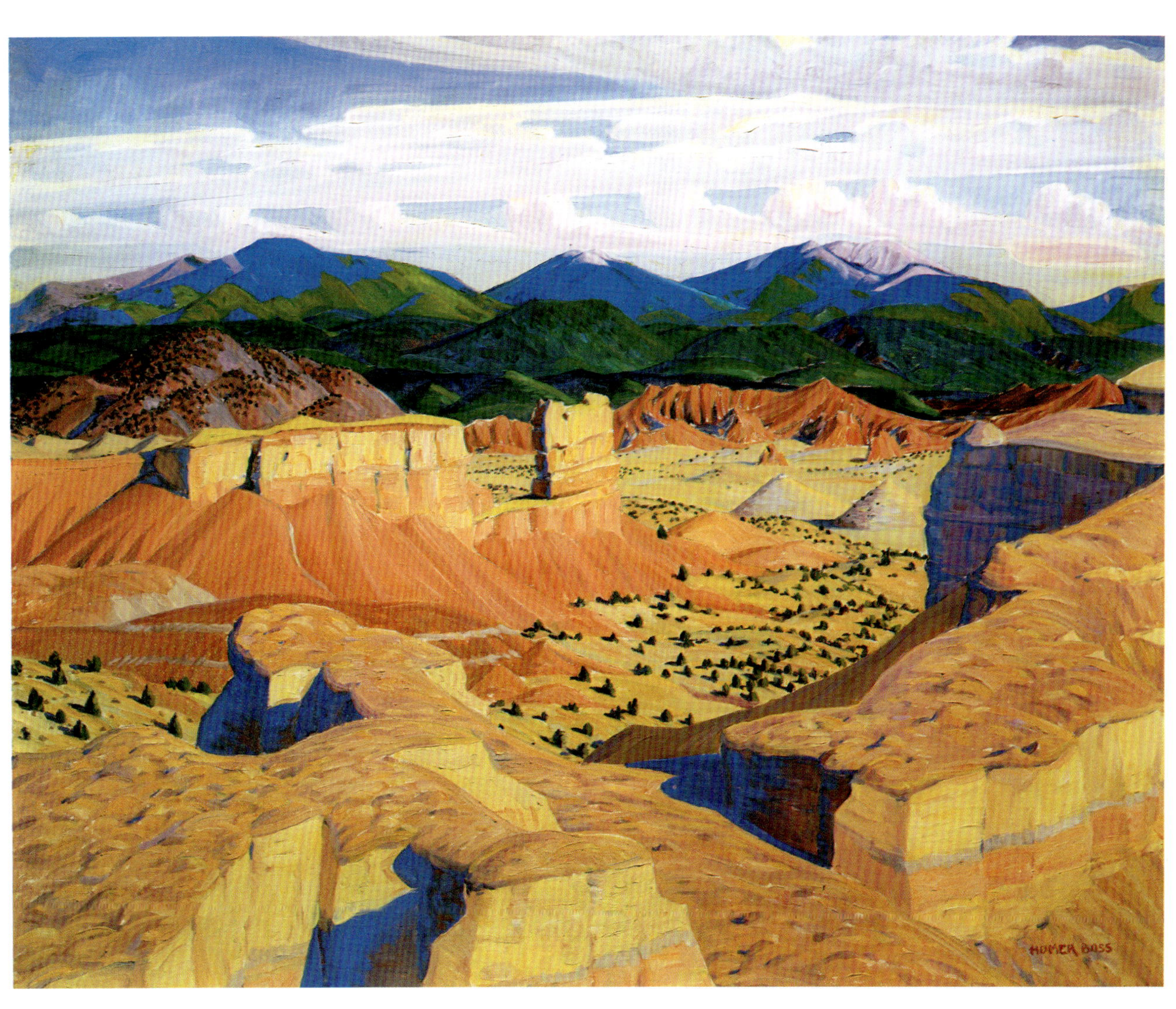

7. Homer Boss, *Red Clay Formation,* oil on canvas, 26 × 32 in.

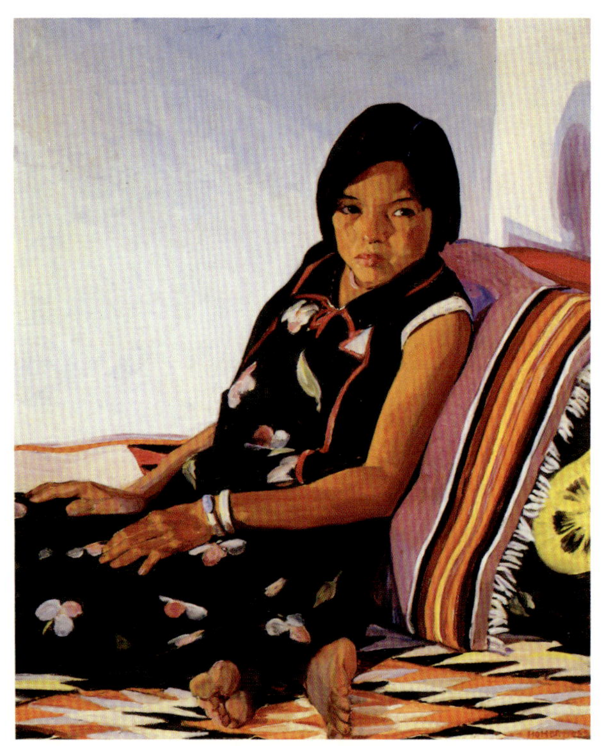

8. Homer Boss, *Nina,* oil on canvas, 32 × 26 in.

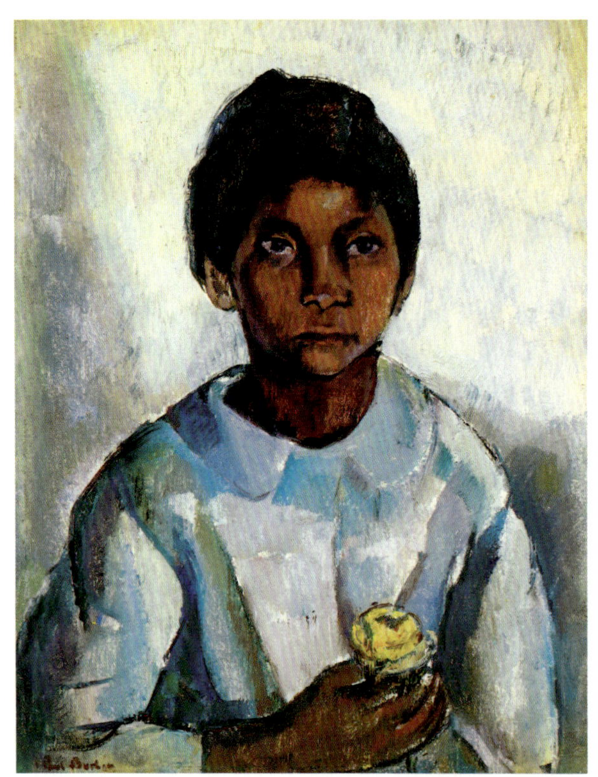

9. Paul Burlin, *Girl with Flower,* oil on masonite, 18 × 14 in.

40

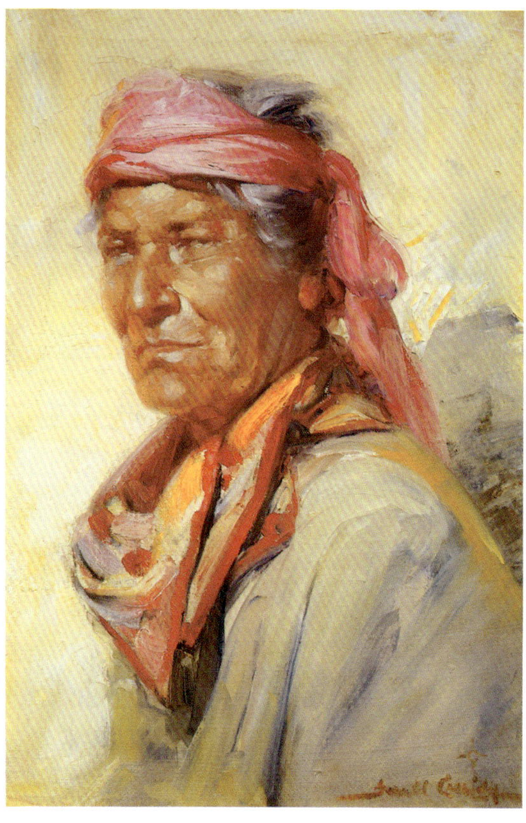

10. Gerald Cassidy, *Big Mike the Apache,* oil on canvas, 24 × 16 in.

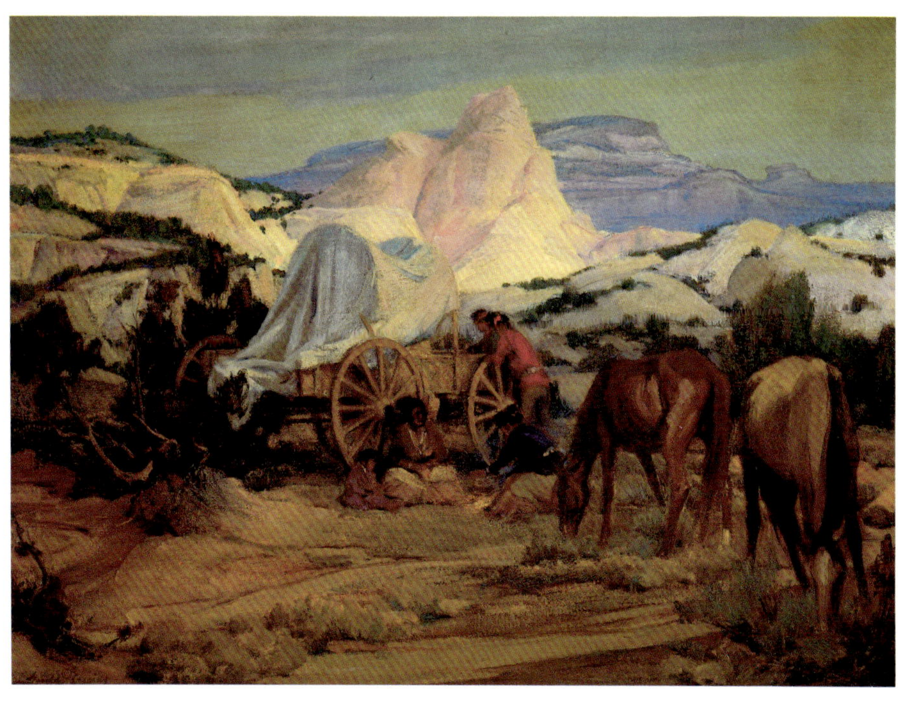

11. Gerald Cassidy, *Evening Meal, Navajo Land,* oil on canvas, 30 × 40 in.

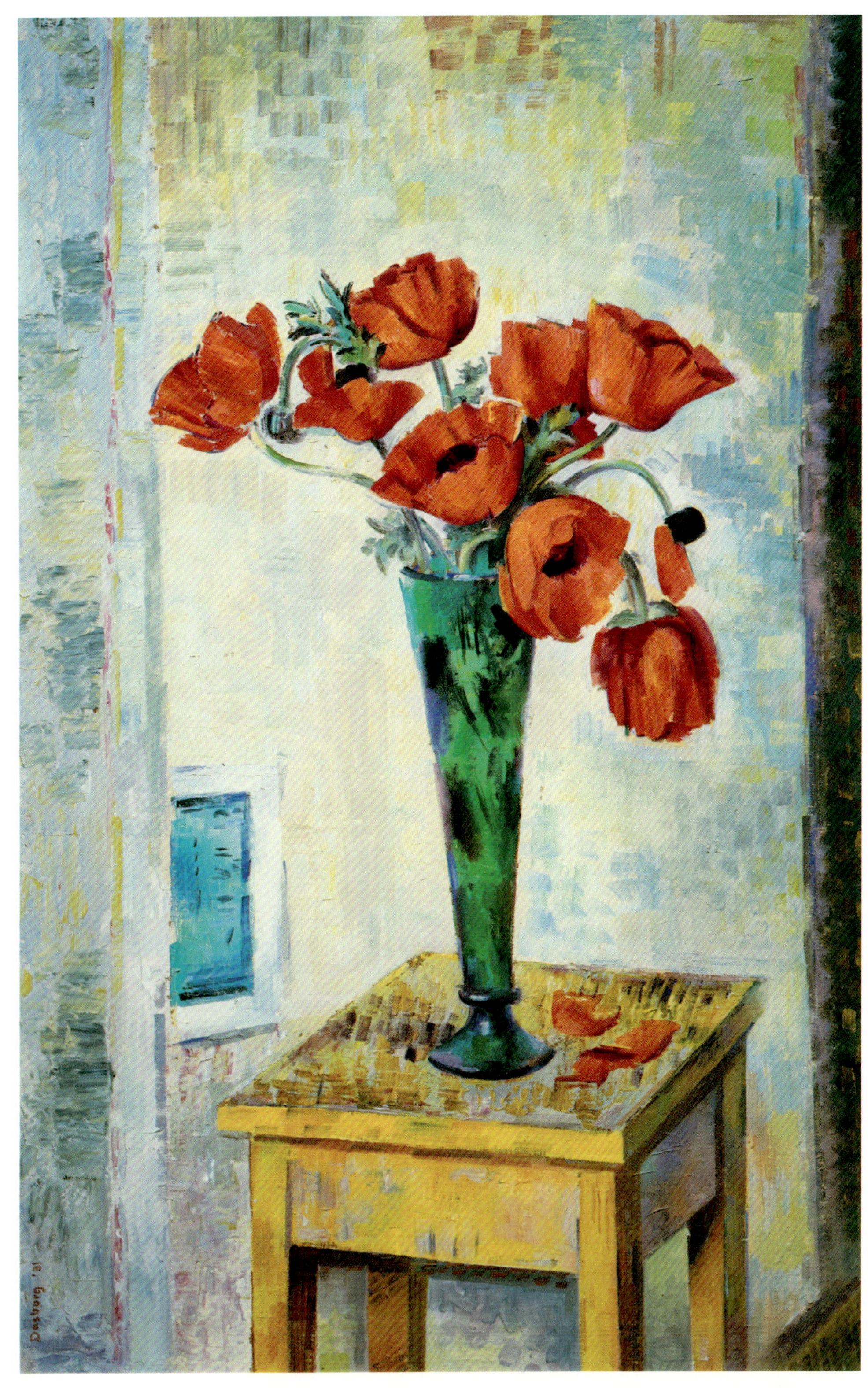

12. Andrew Dasburg, *Still Life (Poppies)*, oil on canvas, 40-1/2 × 26-1/4 in.

42

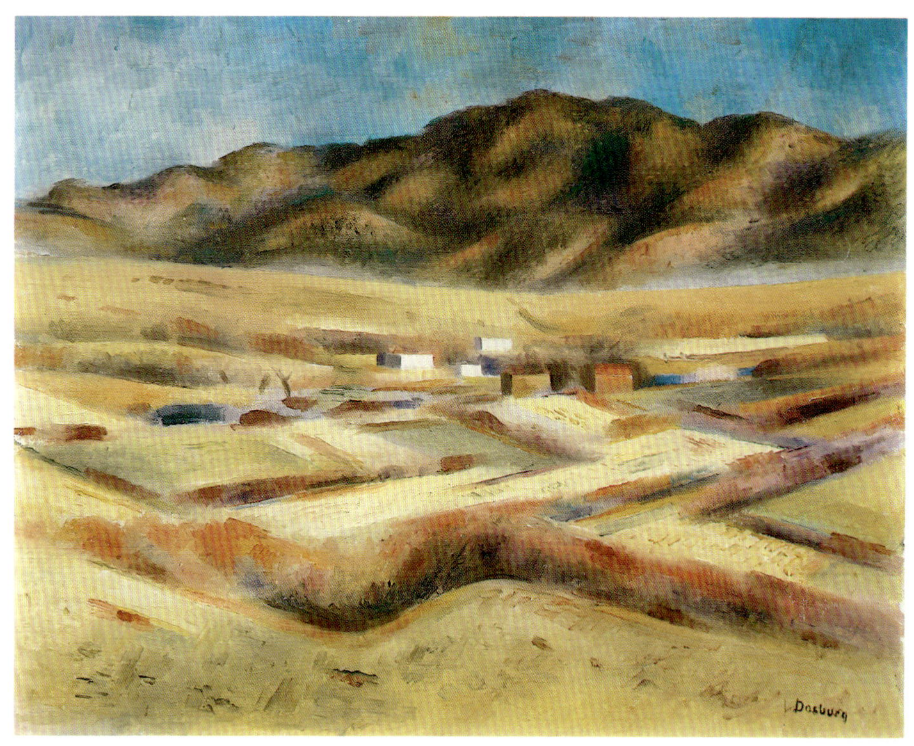

13. Andrew Dasburg, *Taos Scene,* oil on canvas, 12-1/2 × 15-1/2 in.

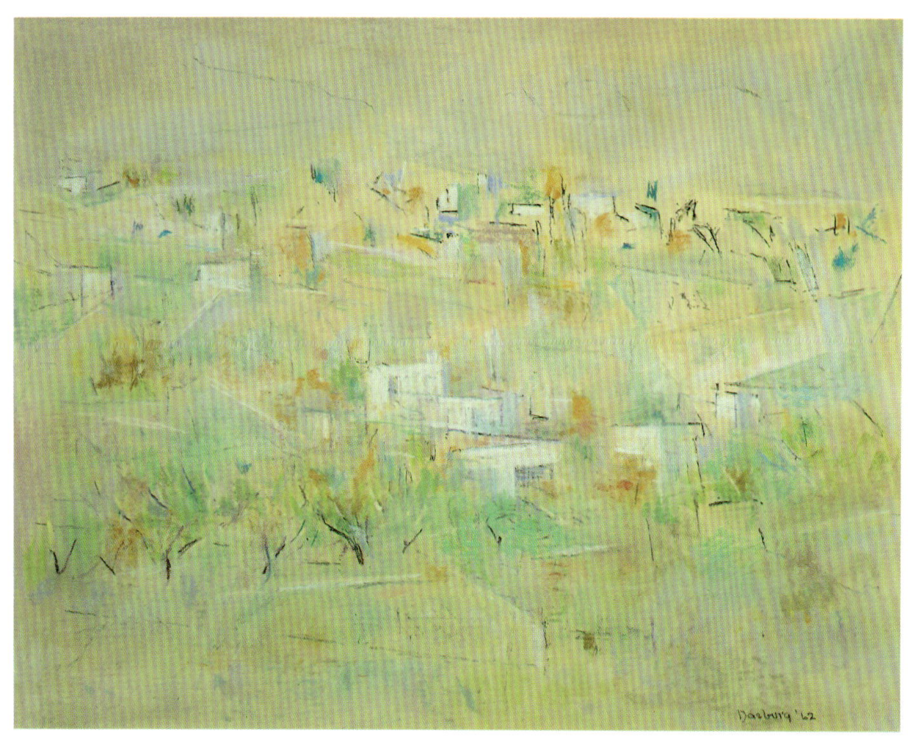

14. Andrew Dasburg, *October Landscape,* 1962, pastel, 17-1/2 × 22-1/2 in.

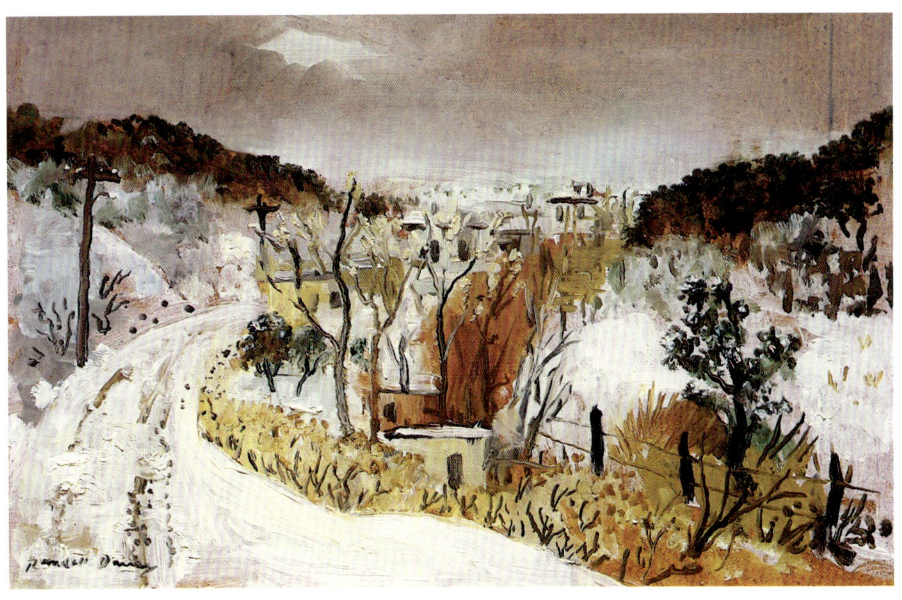

15. Randall Davey, *Upper Canyon Road,* oil on panel, 8 × 12 in.

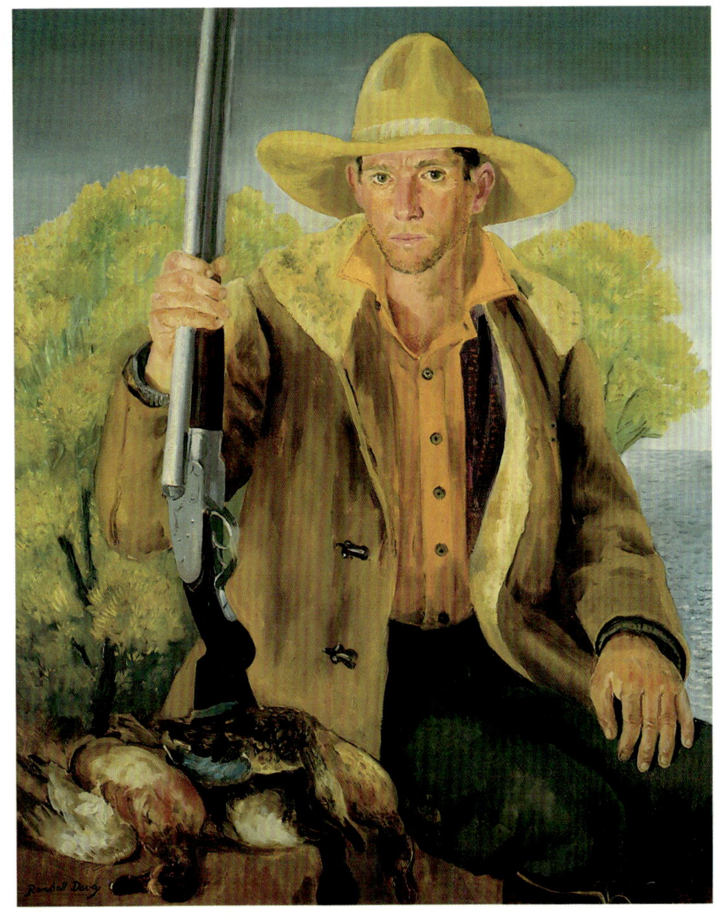

16. Randall Davey, *The Hunter (Johnny Lynch),* oil on canvas, 40-1/8 × 32-1/8 in.

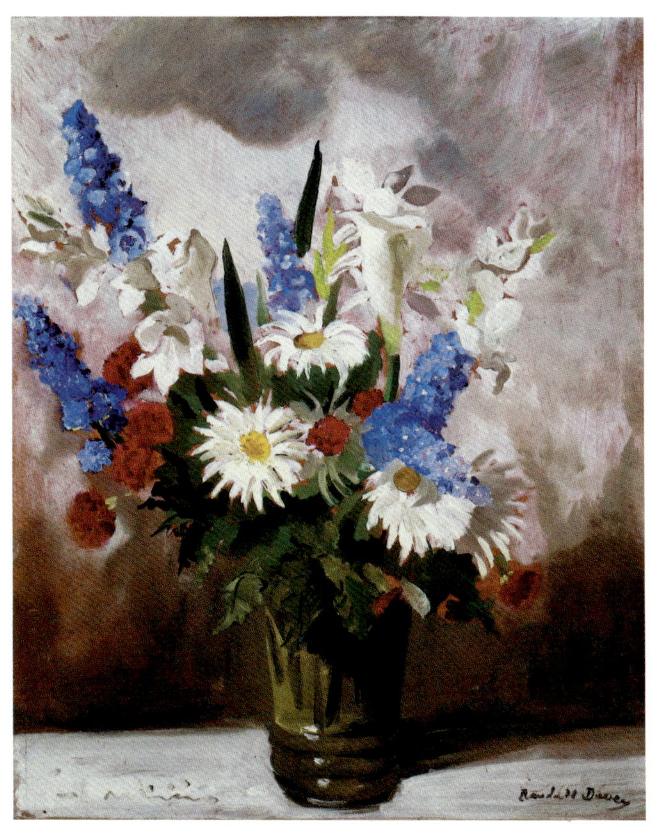

18. Randall Davey, *Flowers on a Marble Table,* oil on masonite, 26 × 31-1/4 in.

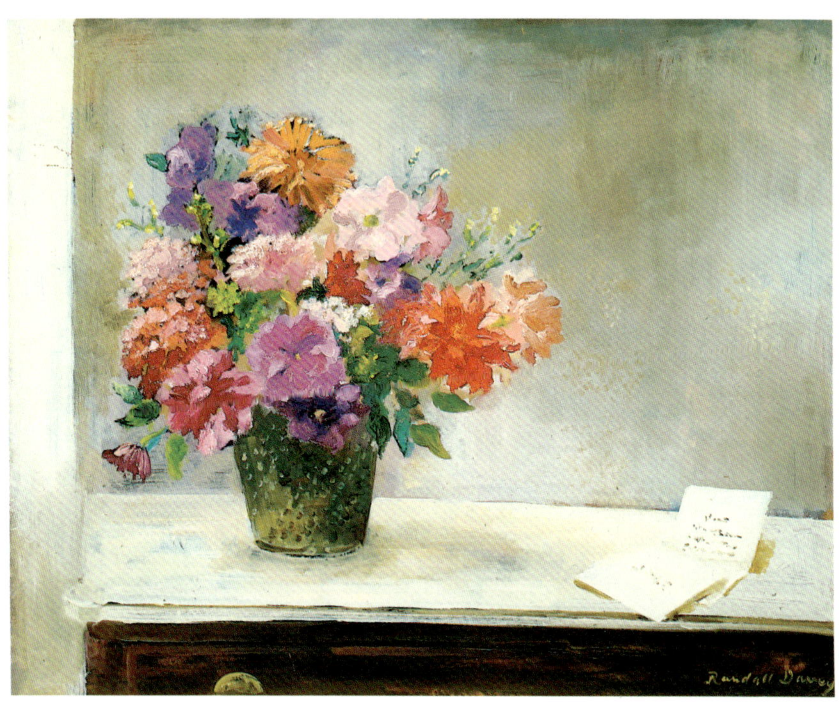

17. Randall Davey, *Still Life— Flowers in a Vase,* 1950, oil on masonite, 32 × 36 in.

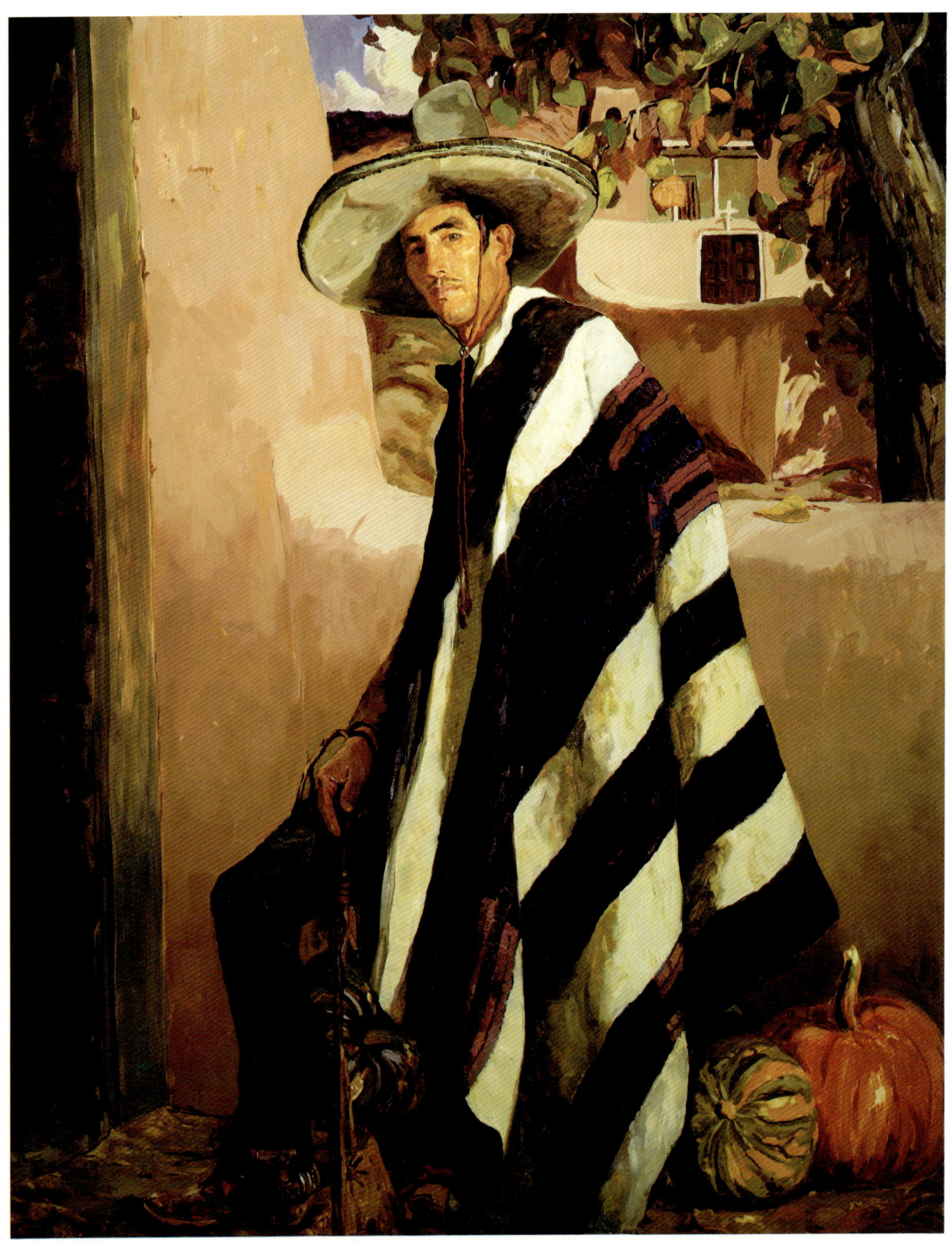

19. Fremont Ellis, *El Caballero*, oil on canvas, 60 × 72 in.

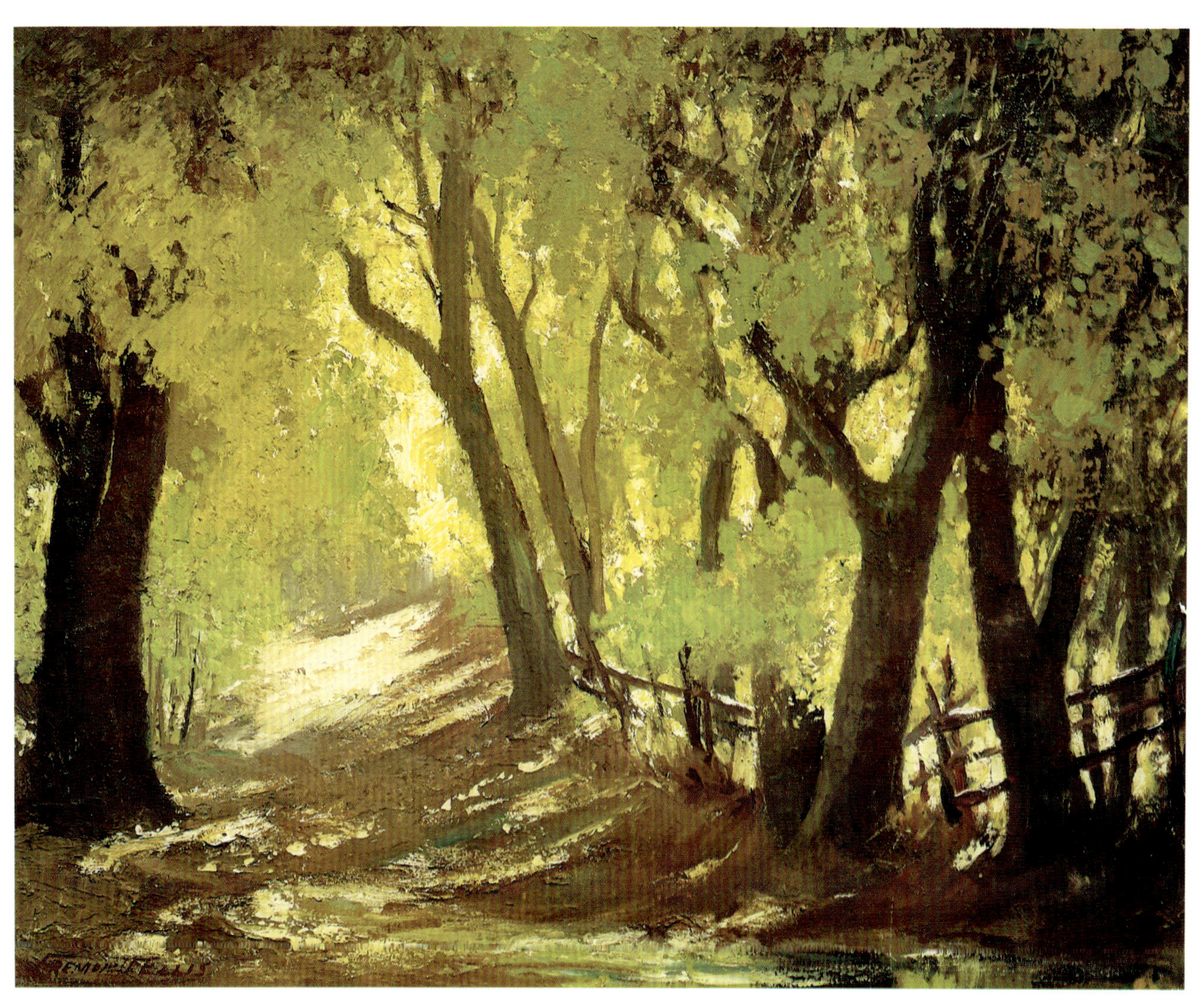

20. Fremont Ellis, *Road Through Cottonwoods,* oil on panel, 13-1/2 × 9-1/2 in.

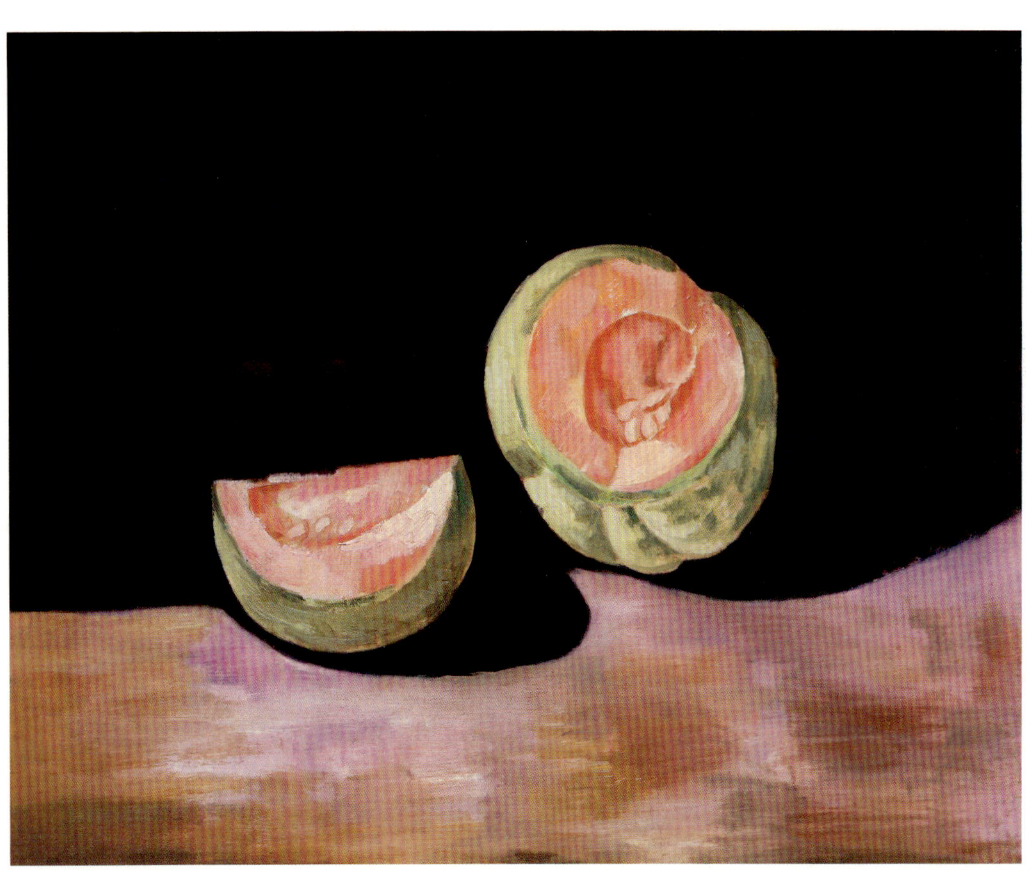

21. Marsden Hartley, *Cantaloupe*, 1927–29, oil on canvas, 20 × 24 in.

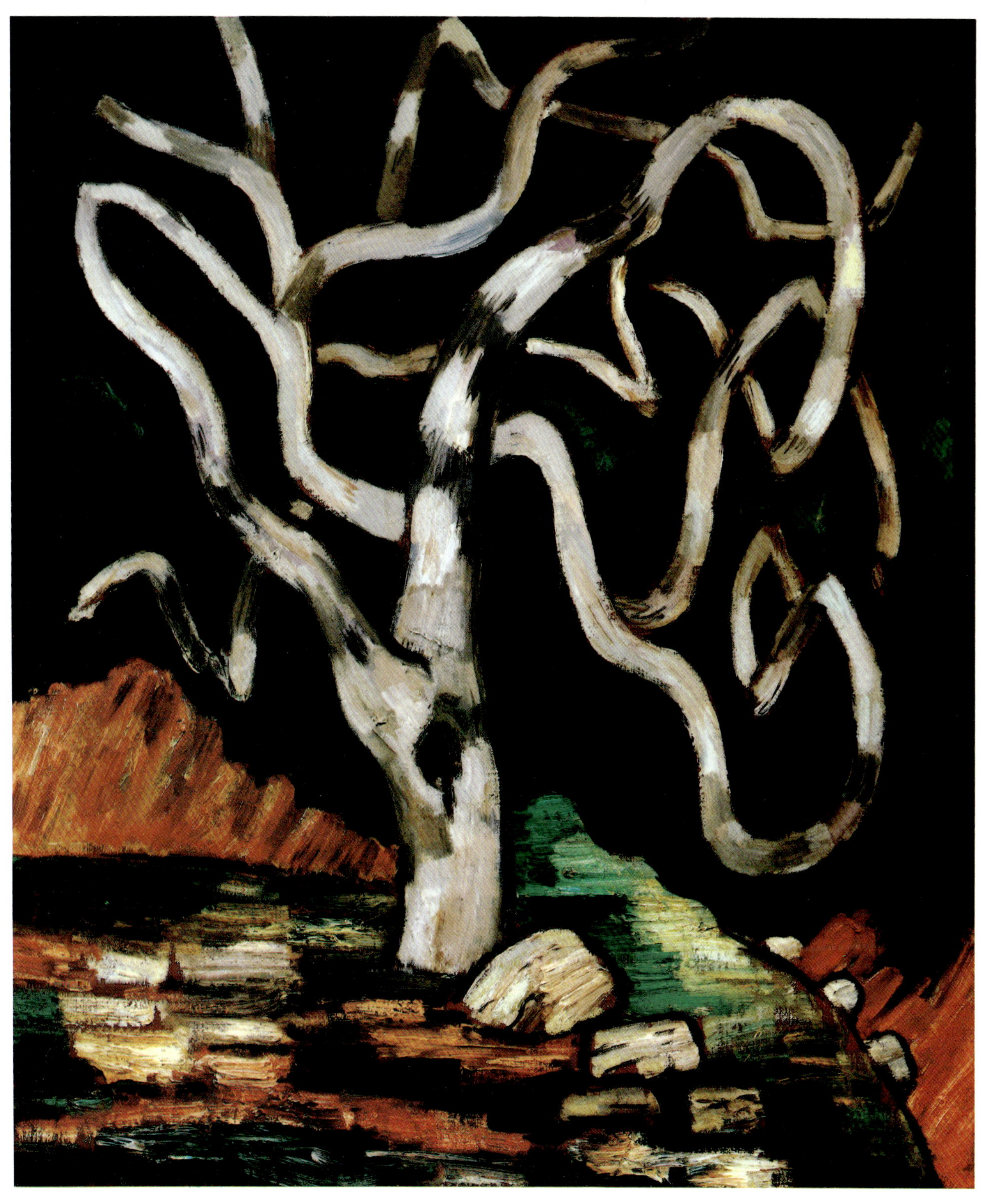

22. Marsden Hartley, *Fig Tree,* oil on canvas, 24-1/2 × 20-1/2 in.

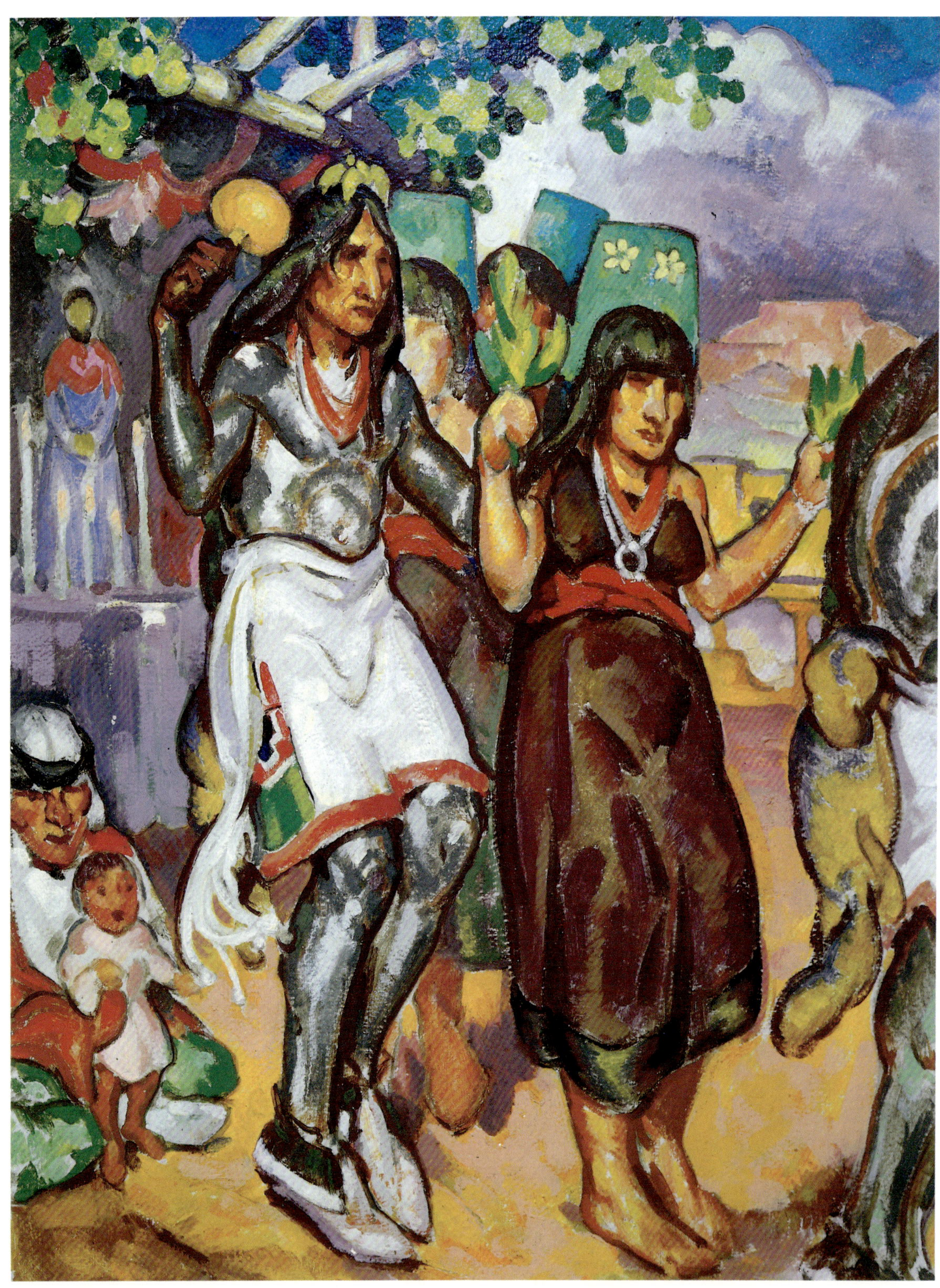

23. William Penhallow Henderson, *Before the Shrine, San Ildefonso,* c. 1920, oil on board, 23-1/2 × 18 in.

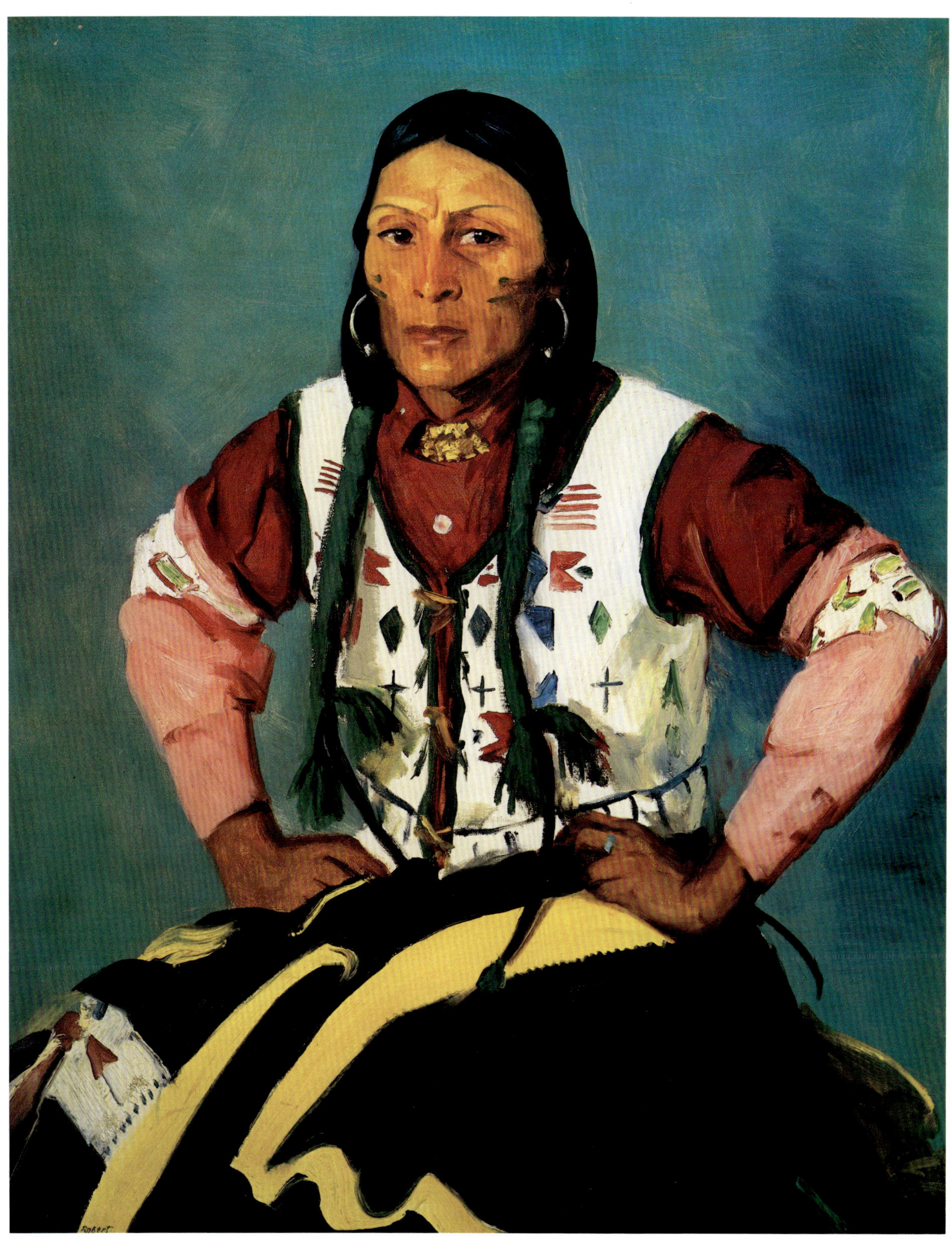

24. Robert Henri, *Portrait of an Indian, Po Tse (Water Eagle)*, oil on canvas, 41-1/2 × 32-3/4 in.

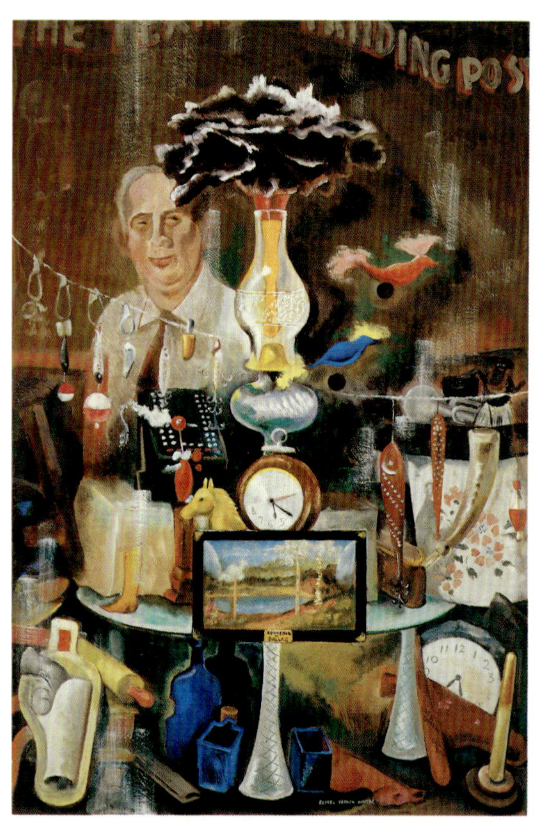

25. Russel Vernon Hunter,
Trading Post, Dallas, 1950, oil
on masonite, 36 × 23-3/4 in.

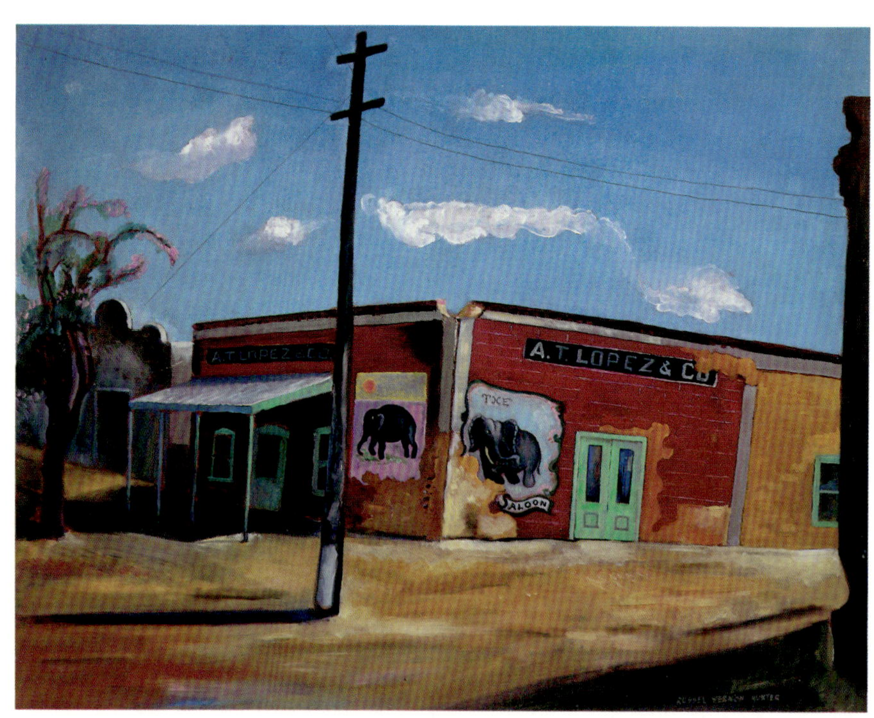

26. Russel Vernon Hunter,
American Mural—Old Mesilla,
1936, oil on masonite,
22-1/4 × 28 in.

52

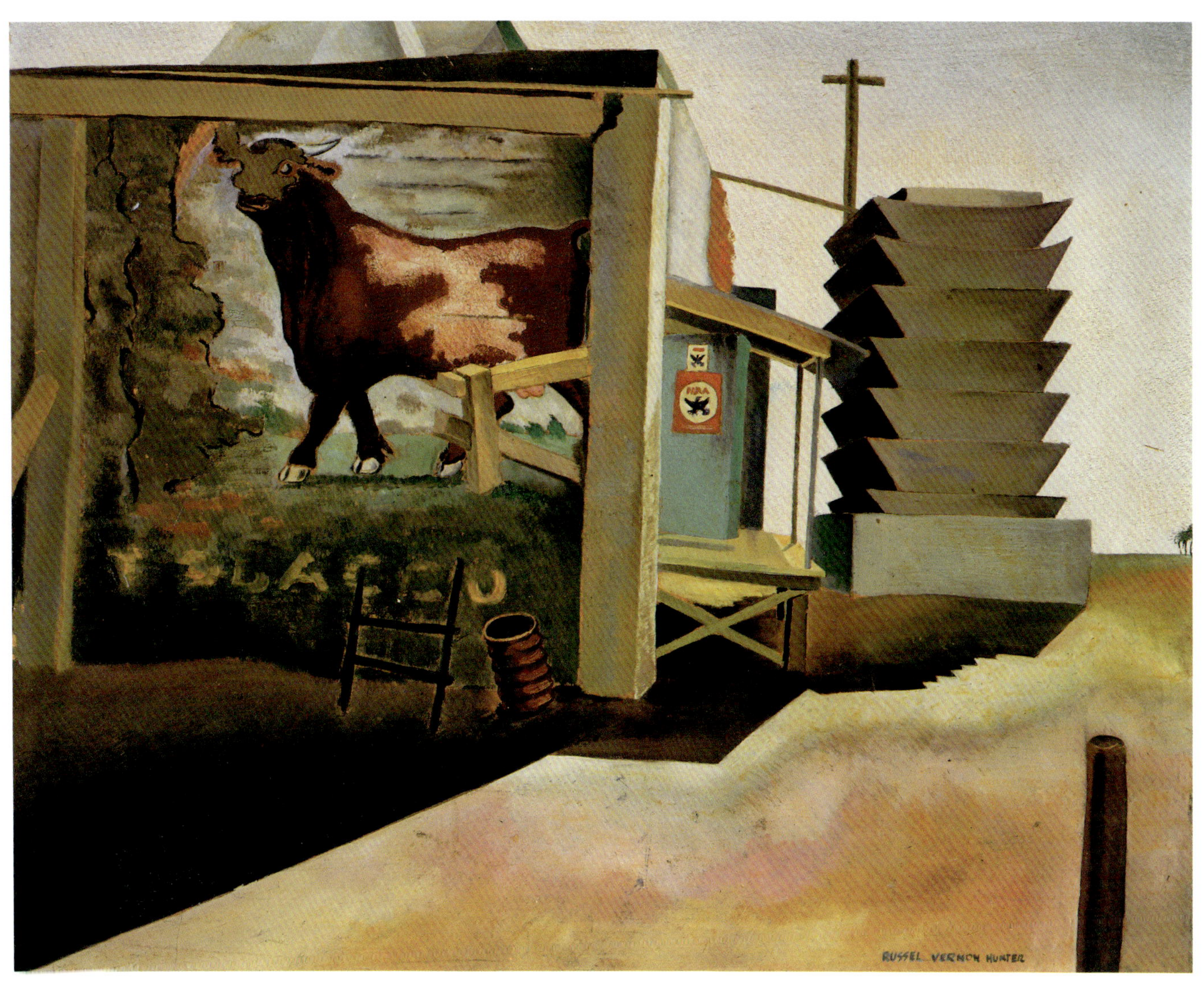

27. Russel Vernon Hunter, *American Mural—Texico, New Mexico*, 1930, oil on masonite, 16 × 19-3/4 in.

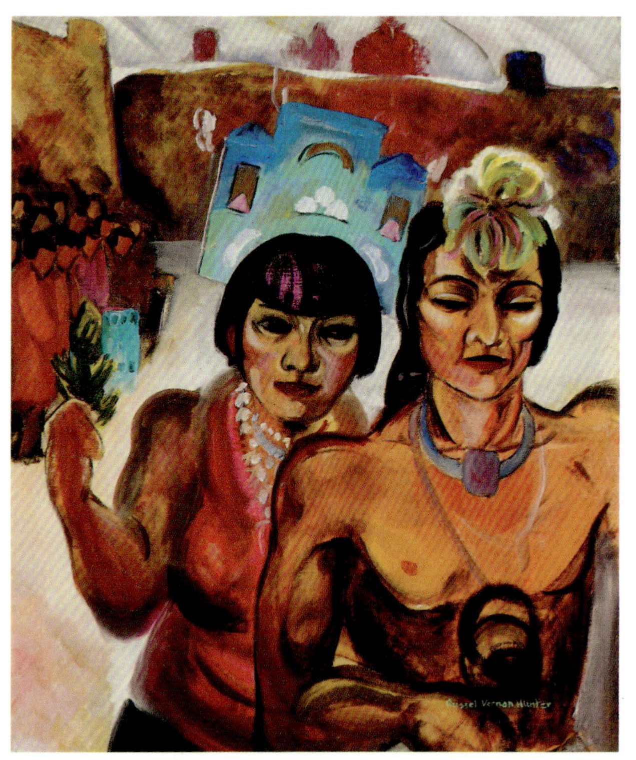

28. Russel Vernon Hunter,
Native Dancers, oil on canvas,
22 × 26 in.

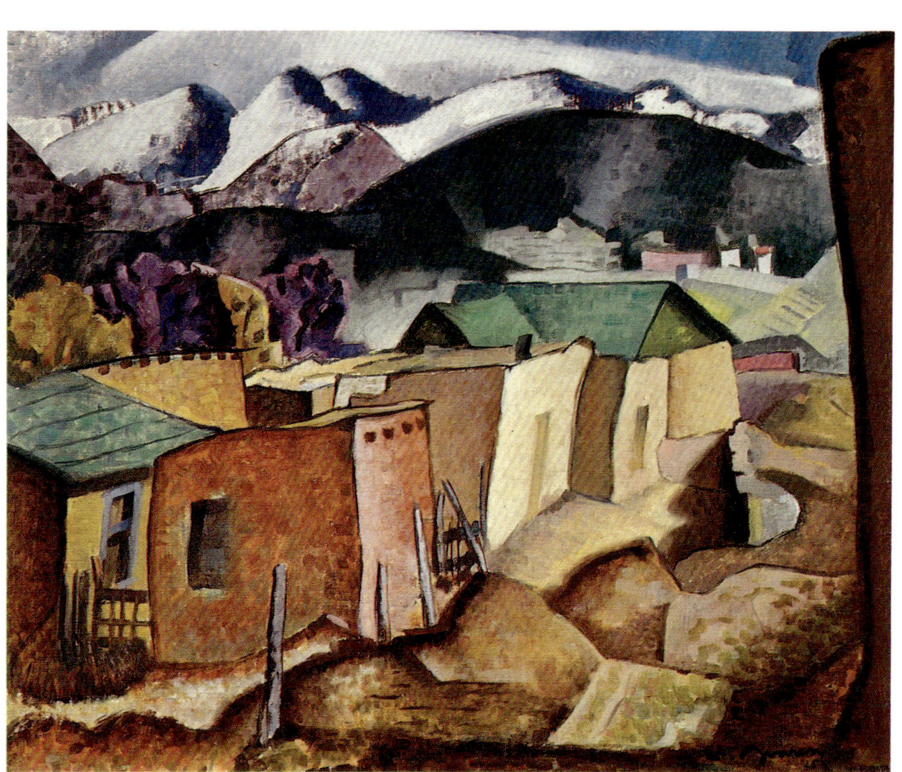

29. Raymond Jonson, *Santa Fe
Placita,* 1925, oil on canvas,
20 × 24 in.

54

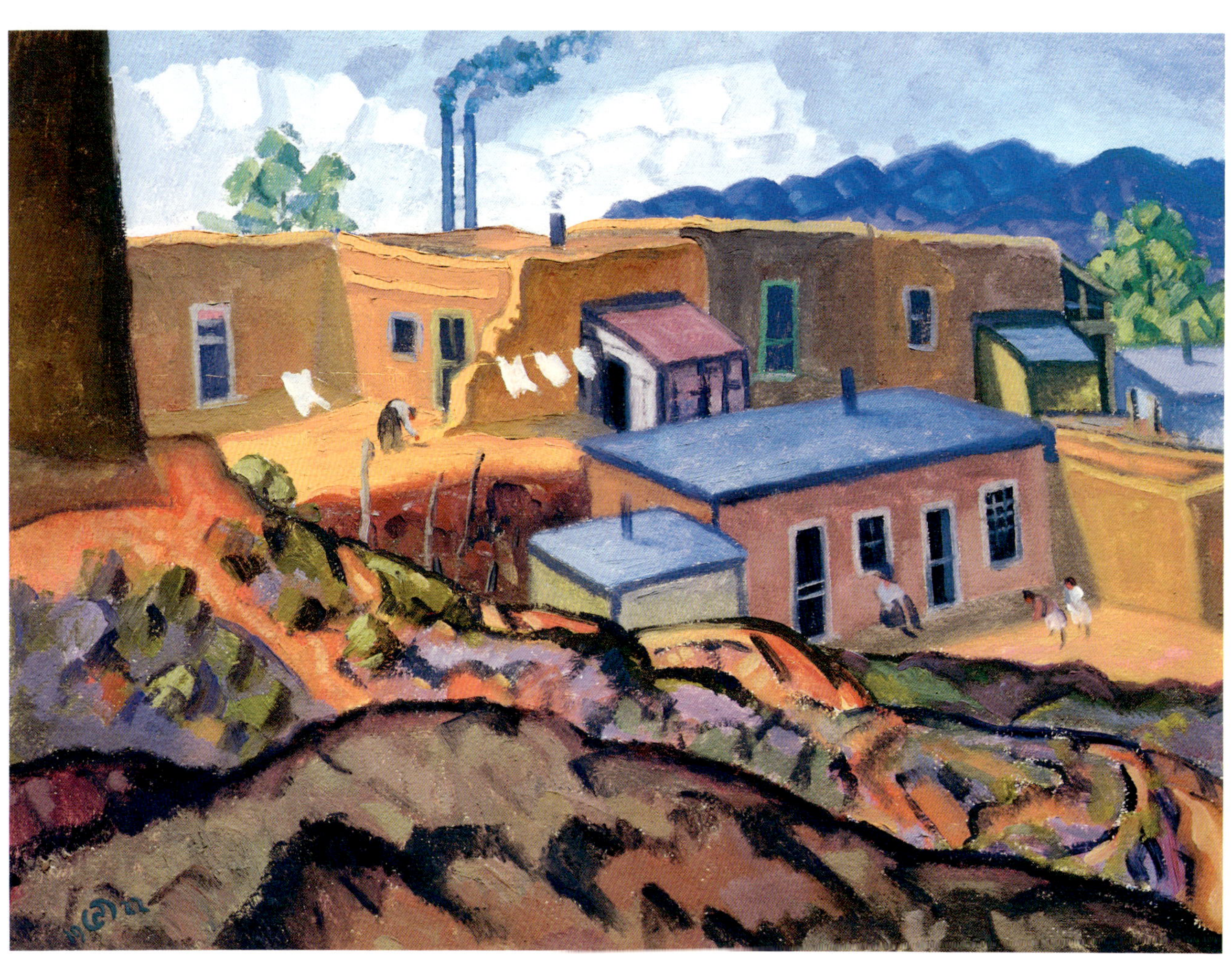

30. Raymond Jonson, *Blue Roofs*, 1922, oil on board, 21 × 27 in.

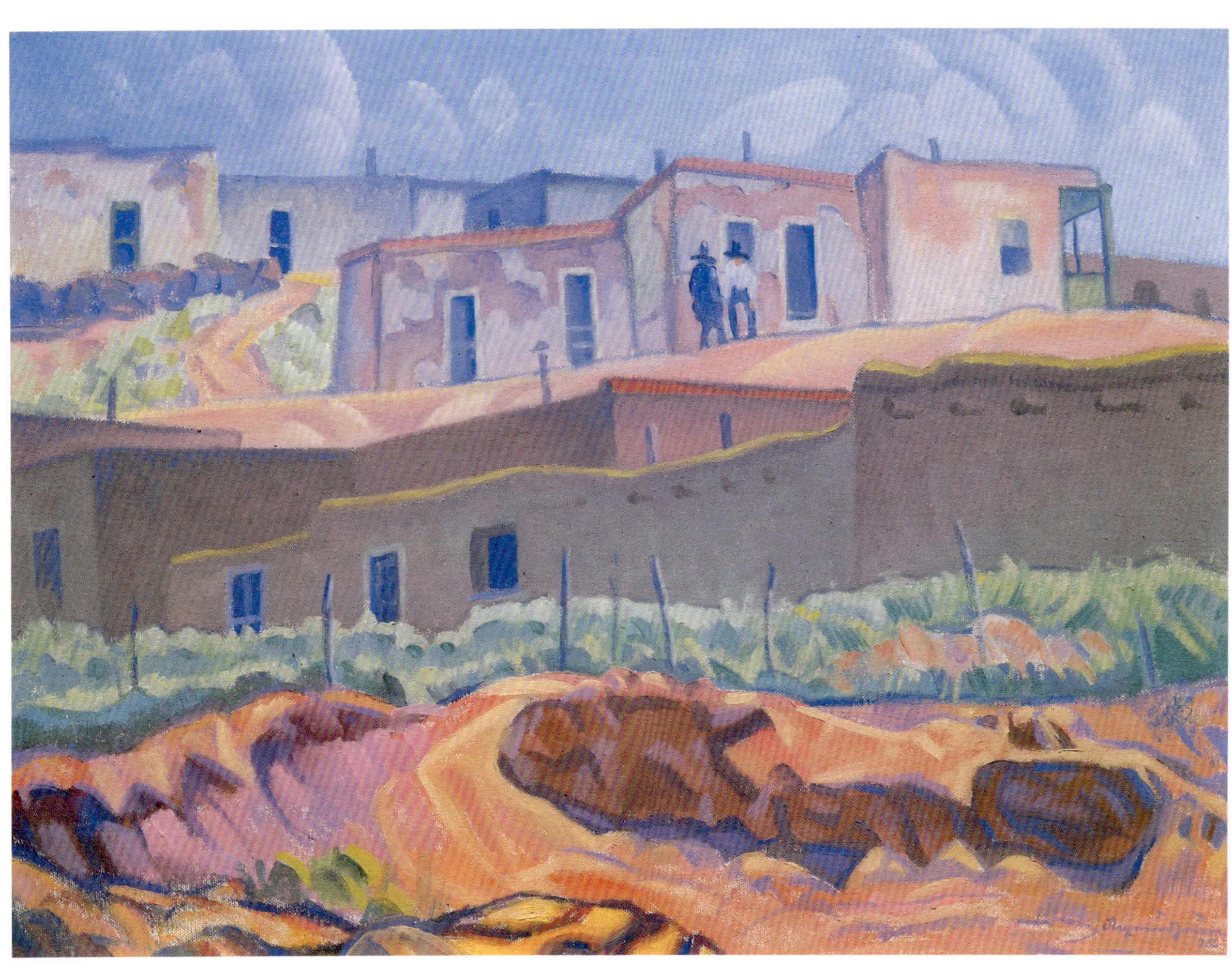

31. Raymond Jonson, *Spanish Quarters,* 1922, oil on canvas, 18 × 24 in.

56

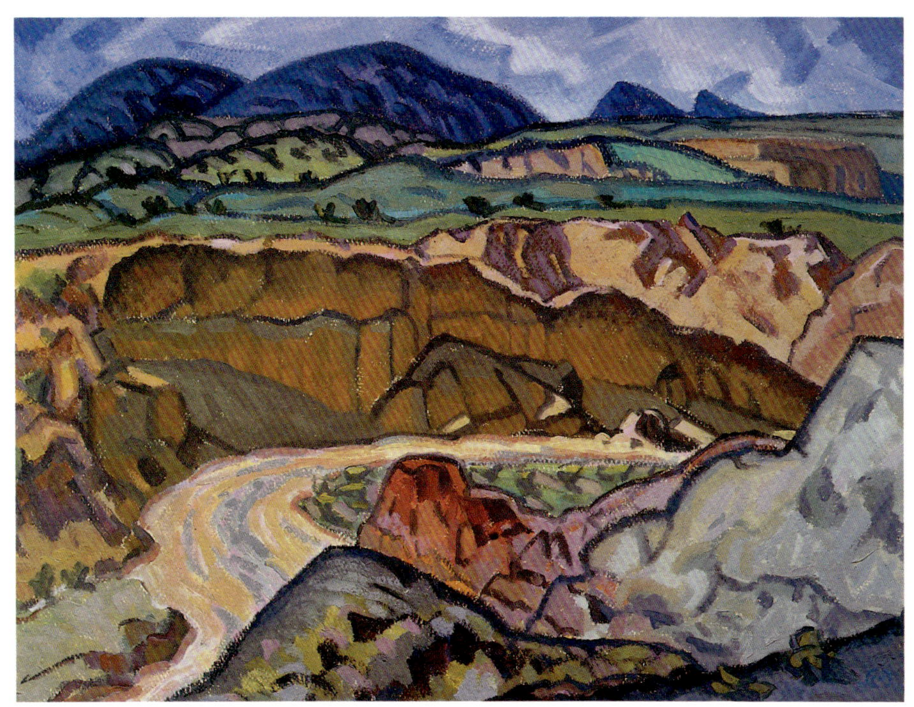

32. Raymond Jonson, *Arroyo, Santa Fe Sketch,* 1922, oil on board, 21 × 27 in.

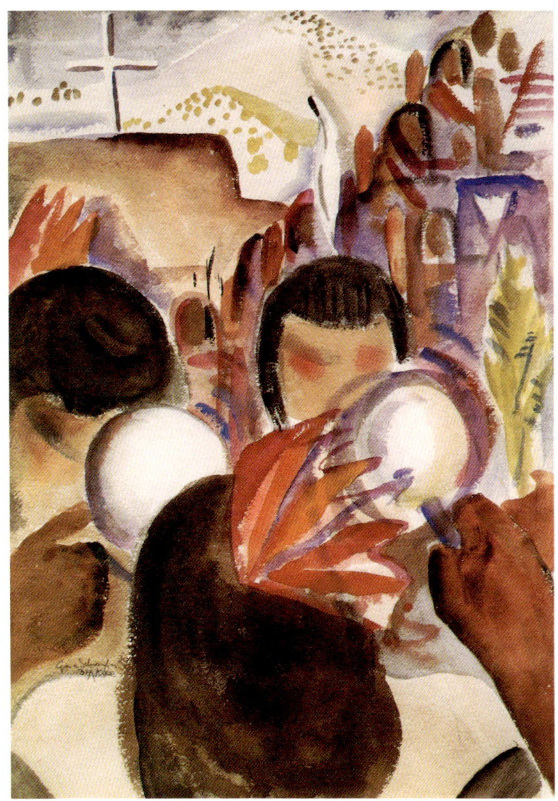

33. Gina Knee, *Corn Dance,* watercolor, 20-1/4 × 14-1/2 in.

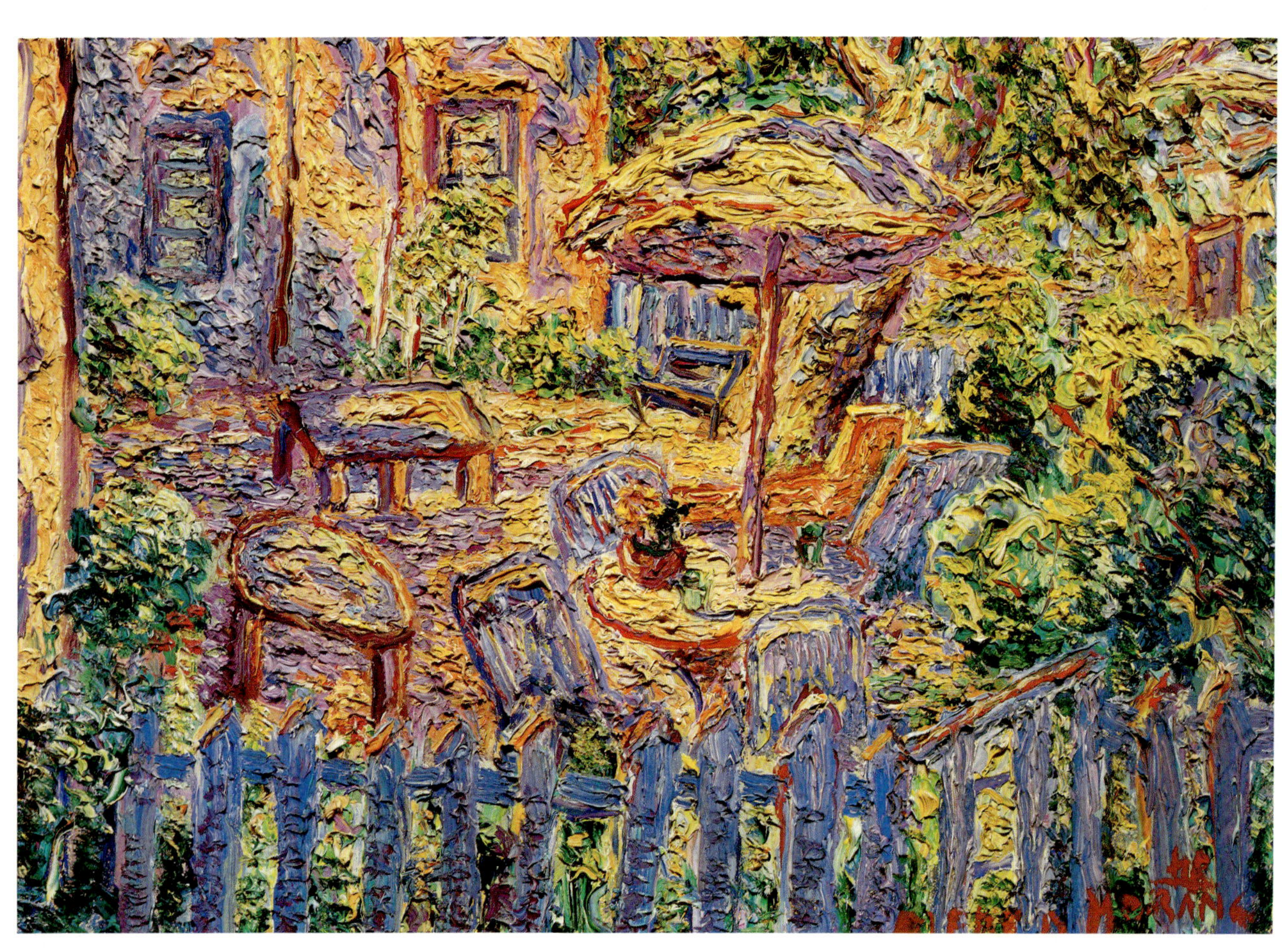

34. Alfred Morang, *Acequia Madre Courtyard*, 1948, oil on canvas, 11 × 15-1/2 in.

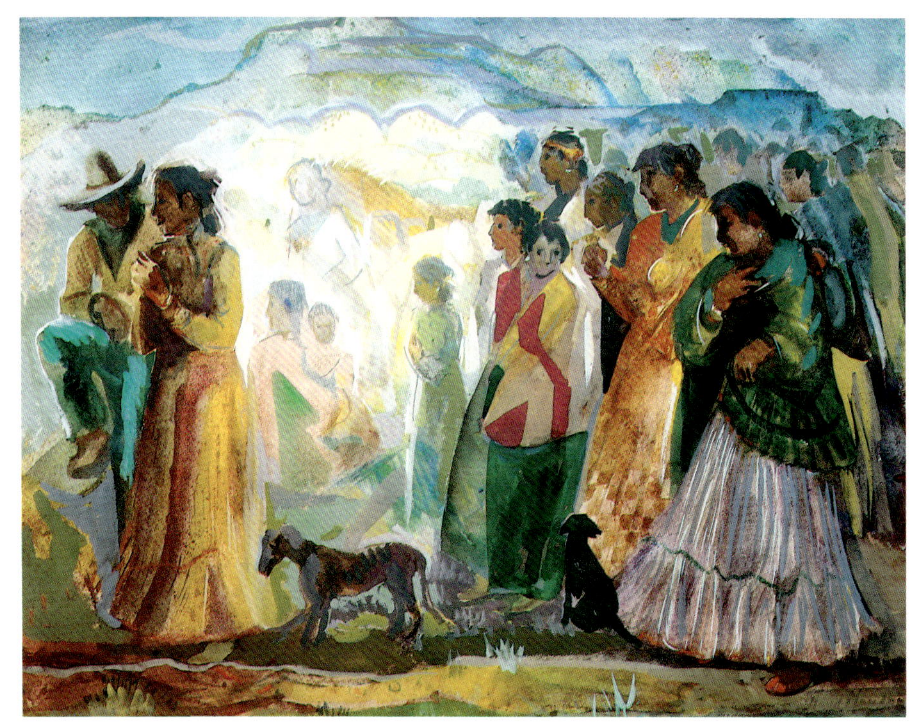

35. Lloyd Moylan, *Indian Ceremonial,* watercolor, 19 × 24-1/2 in.

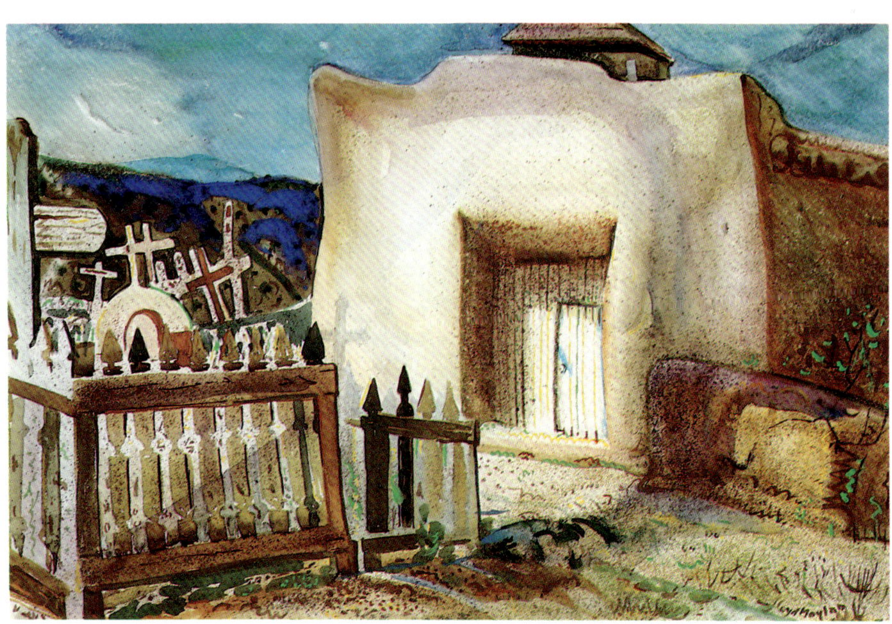

36. Lloyd Moylan, *Adobe Church,* watercolor, 12 × 17-1/2 in.

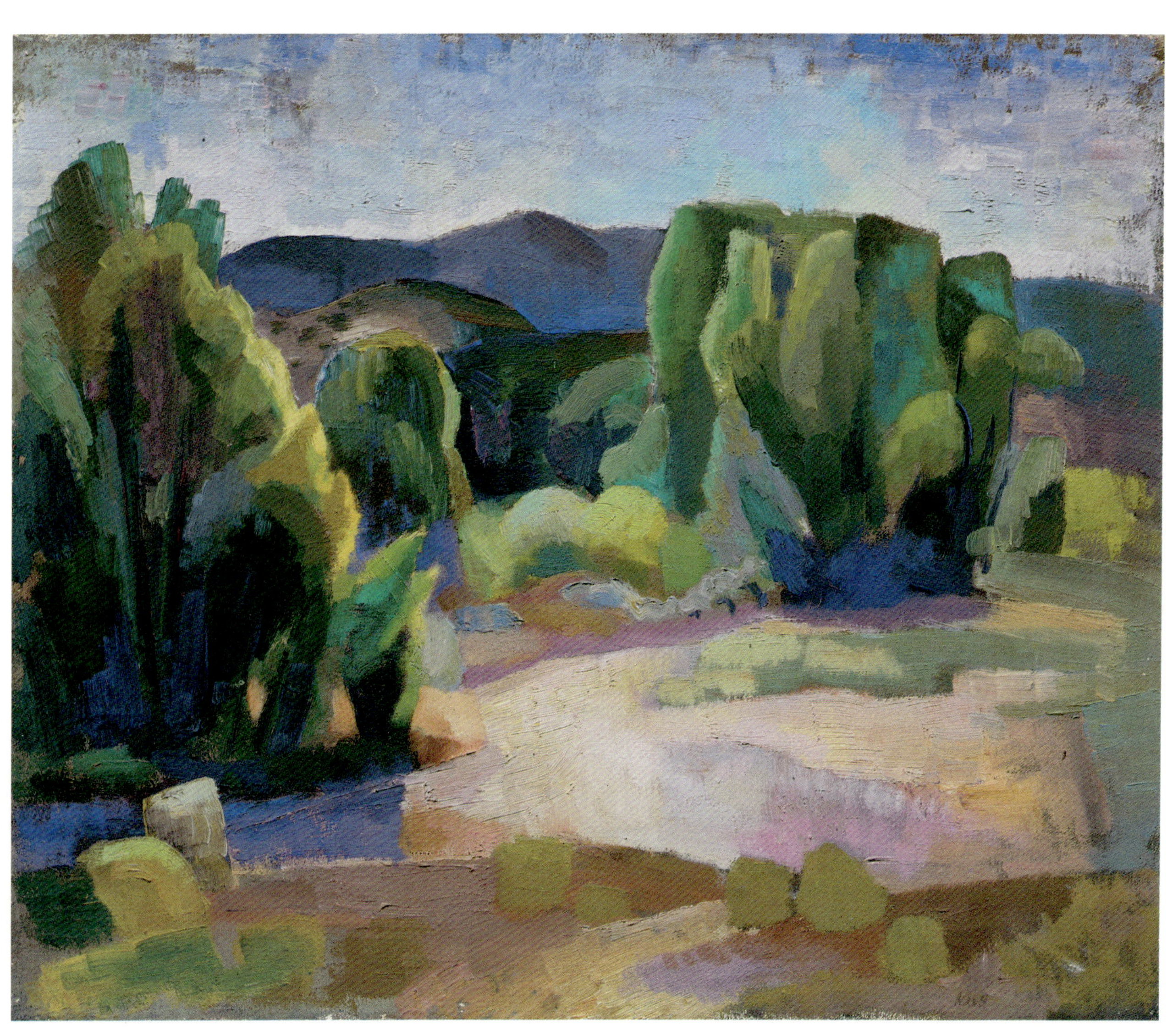

37. Willard Nash, *Landscape,* oil on canvas, 20 × 24 in.

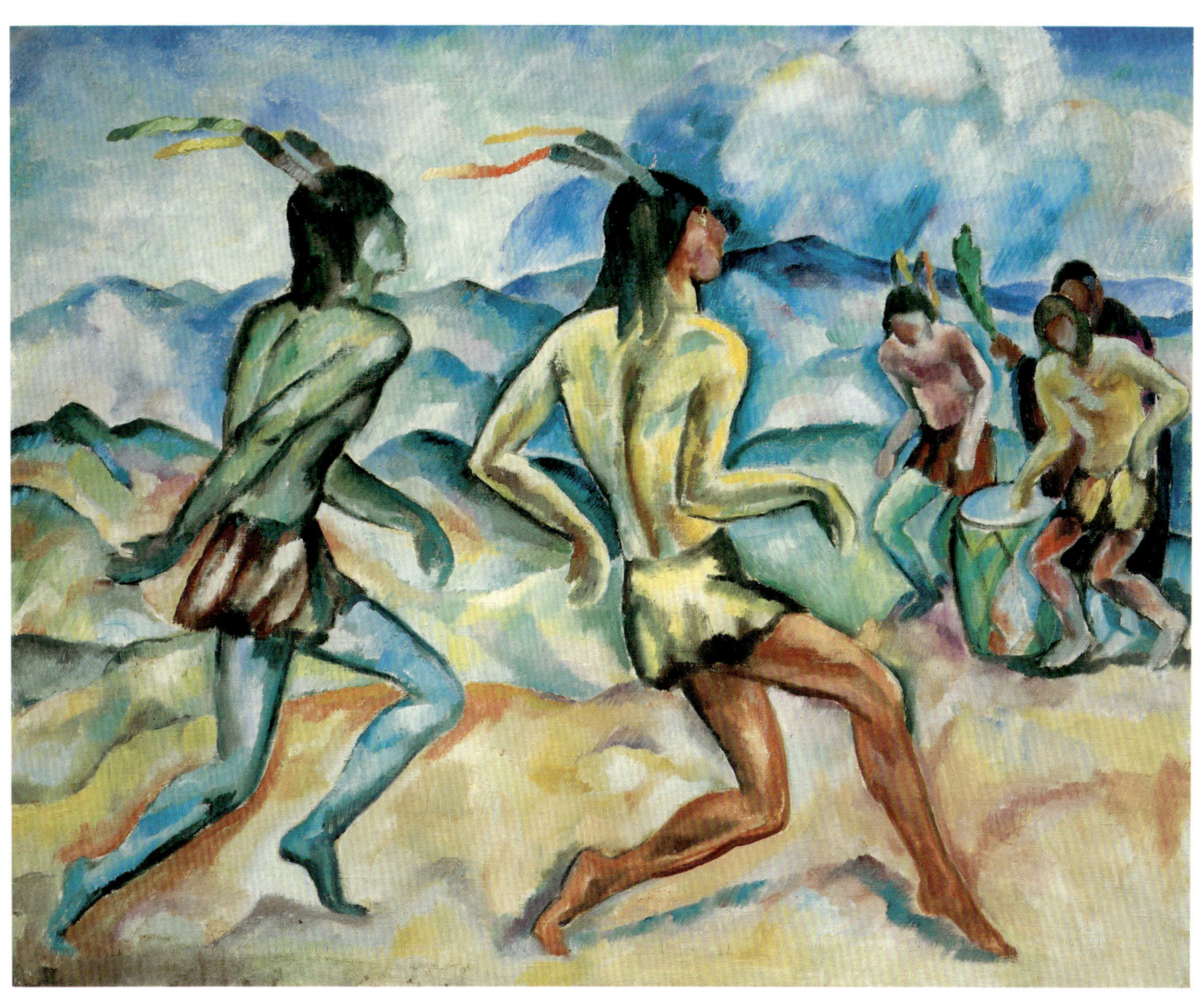

38. B. J. O. Nordfeldt, *Indian Dance (Foot Race—San Juan),* oil on canvas, 29 × 36 in.

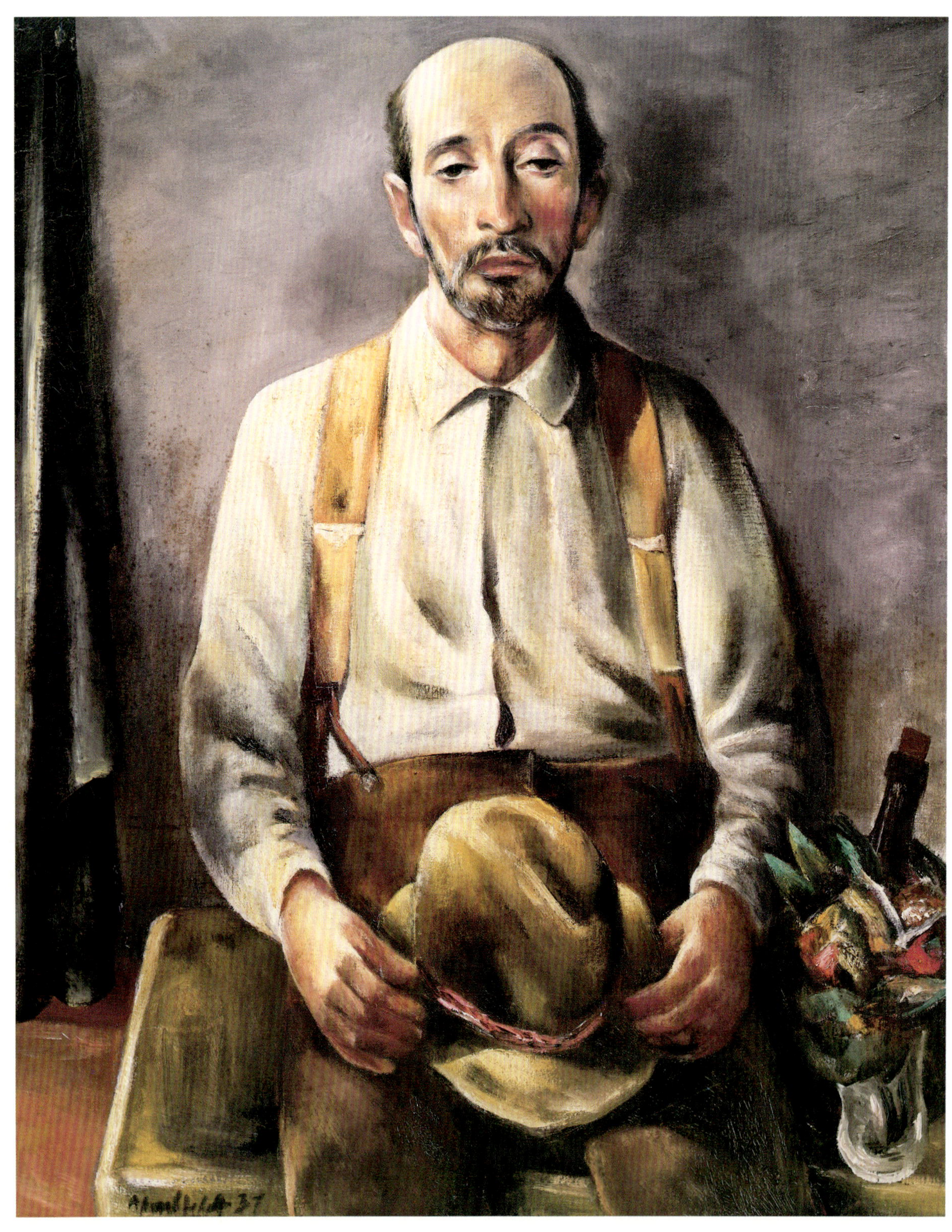

39. B. J. O. Nordfeldt, *Man with Brown Suspenders,* 1937, oil on canvas, 40 × 32 in.

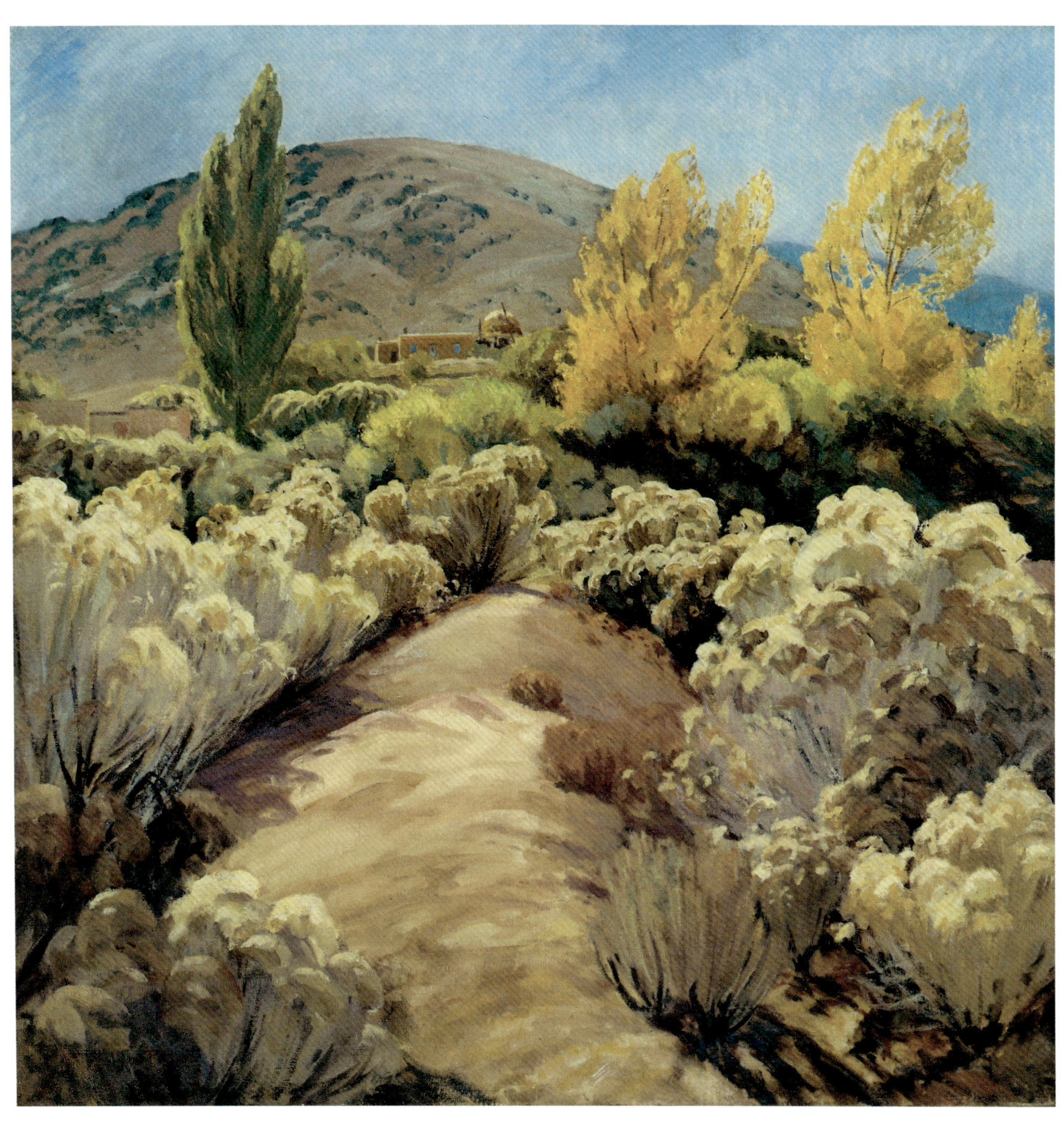

40. Sheldon Parsons, *Chamisa in November,* oil on canvas, 35-1/2 × 35-1/2 in.

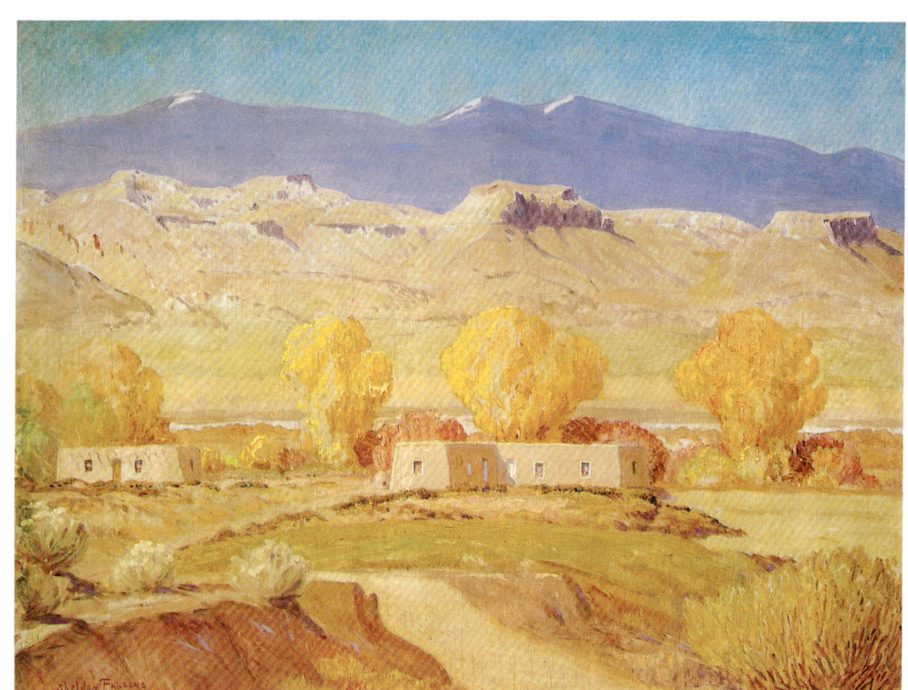

41. Sheldon Parsons, *Near San Ildefonso, New Mexico,* oil on board, 23-1/2 × 31-1/2 in.

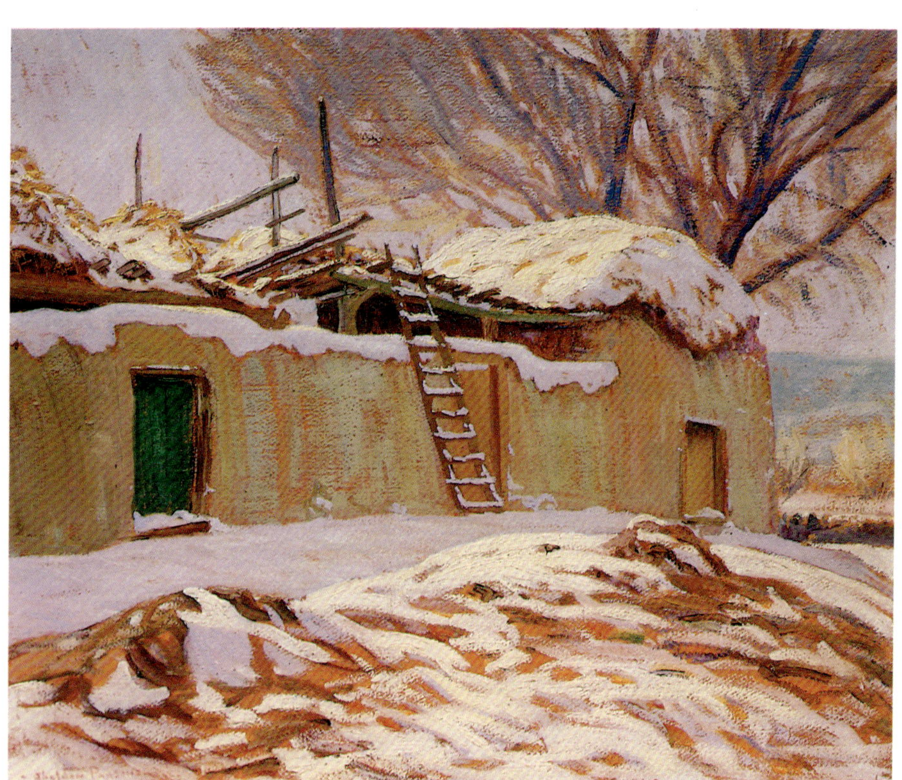

42. Sheldon Parsons, *February in Alcalde,* oil on panel, 20 × 24 in.

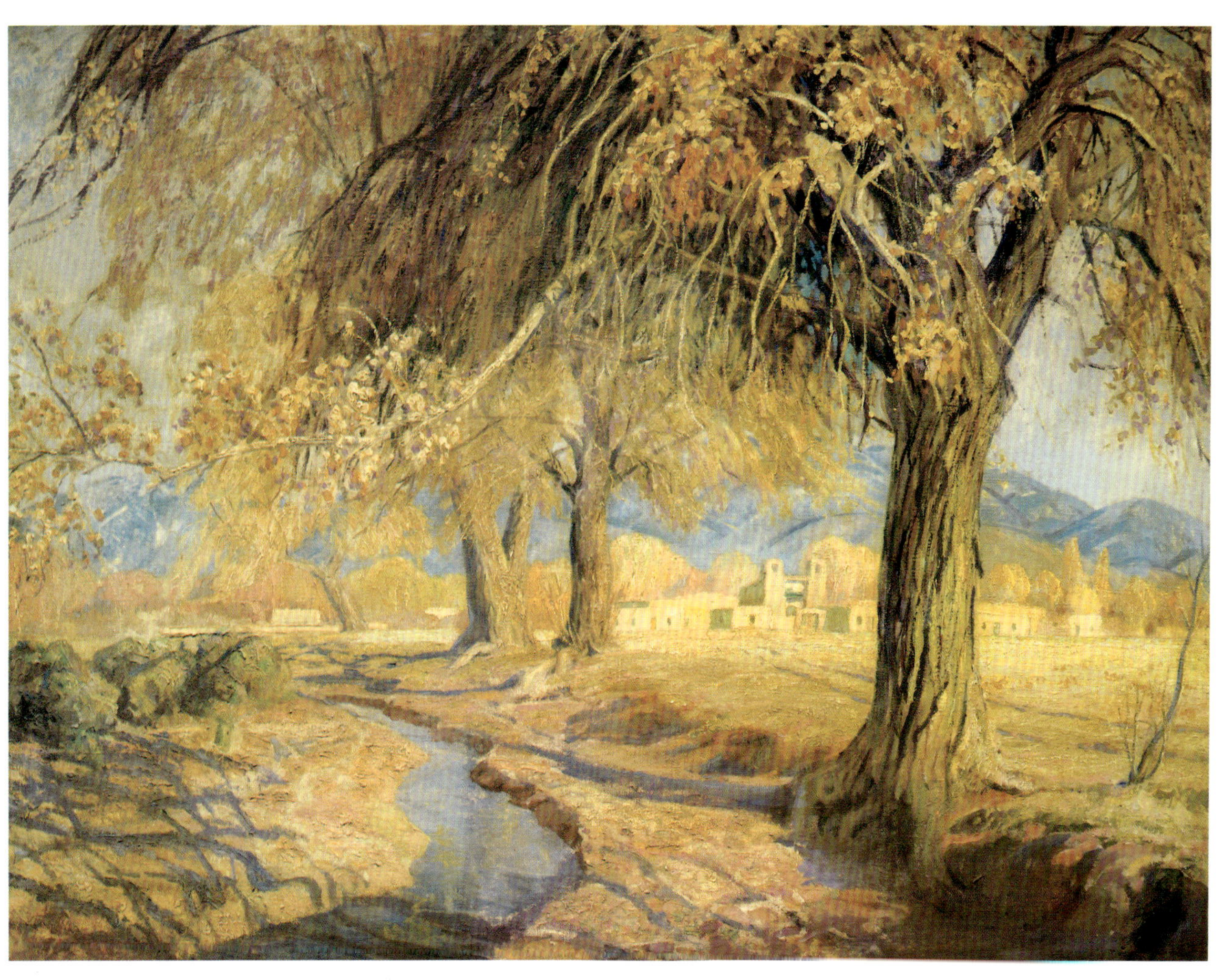

43. Sheldon Parsons, *Pojoaque, New Mexico,* oil on canvas, 38 × 50 in.

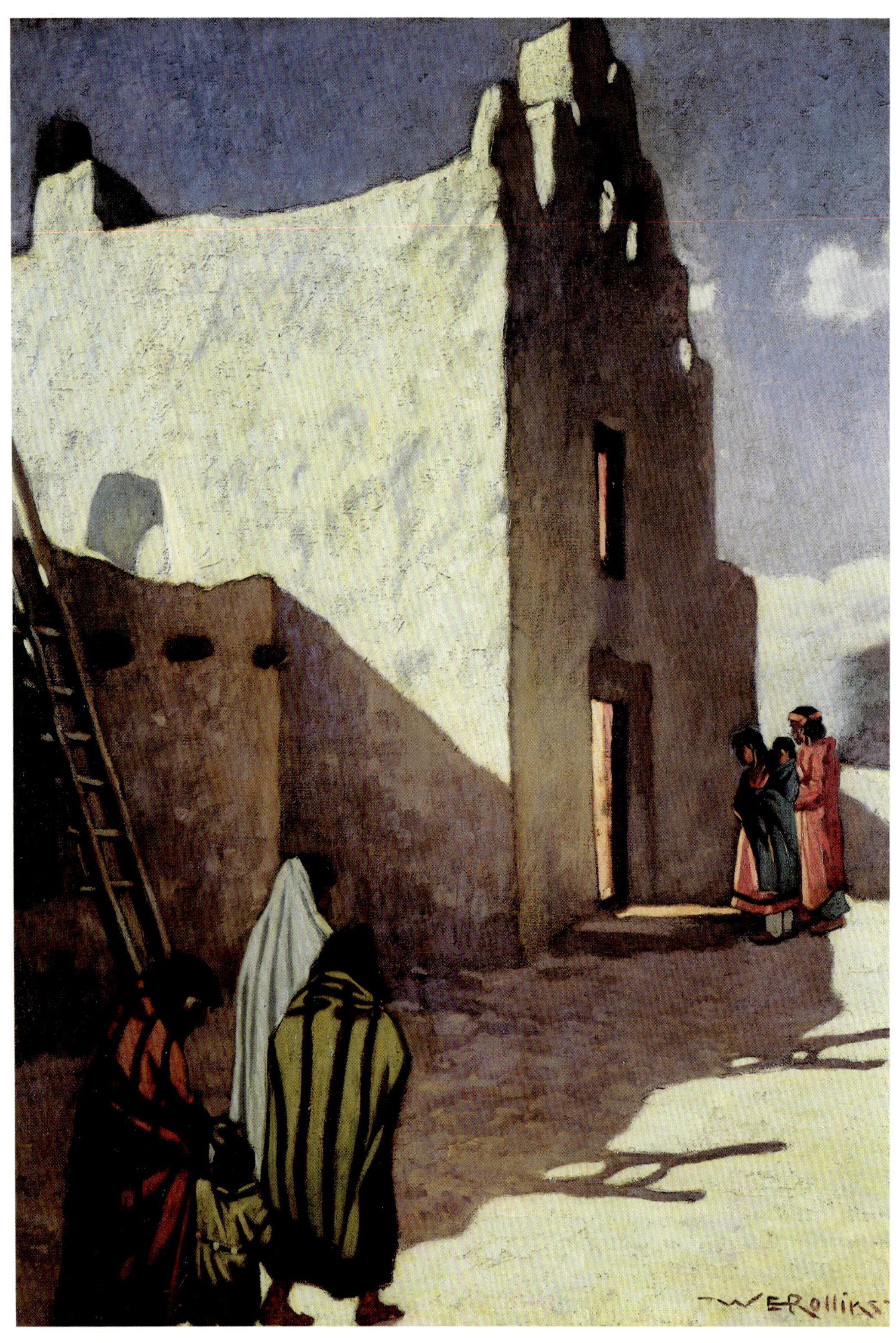

44. Warren Rollins, *House of the Neophytes*, oil on canvas, 41 × 30 in.

66

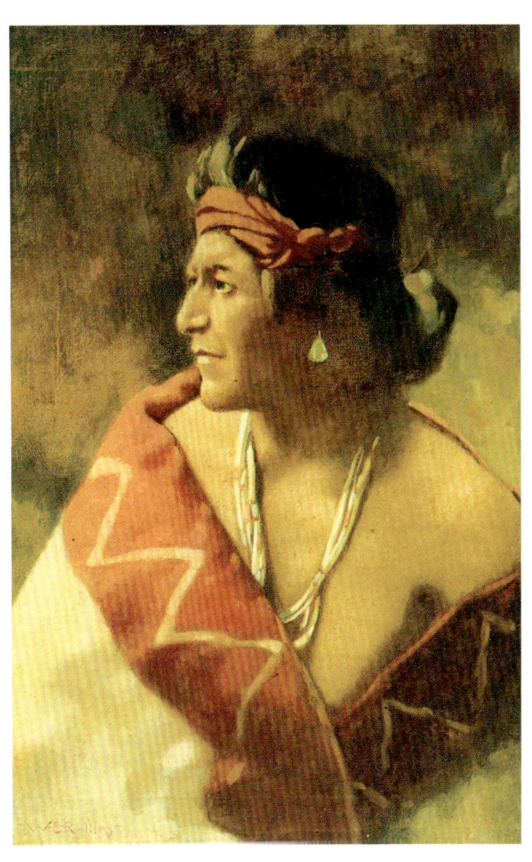

45. Warren Rollins, *The Navajo*, oil on canvas, 28 × 18 in.

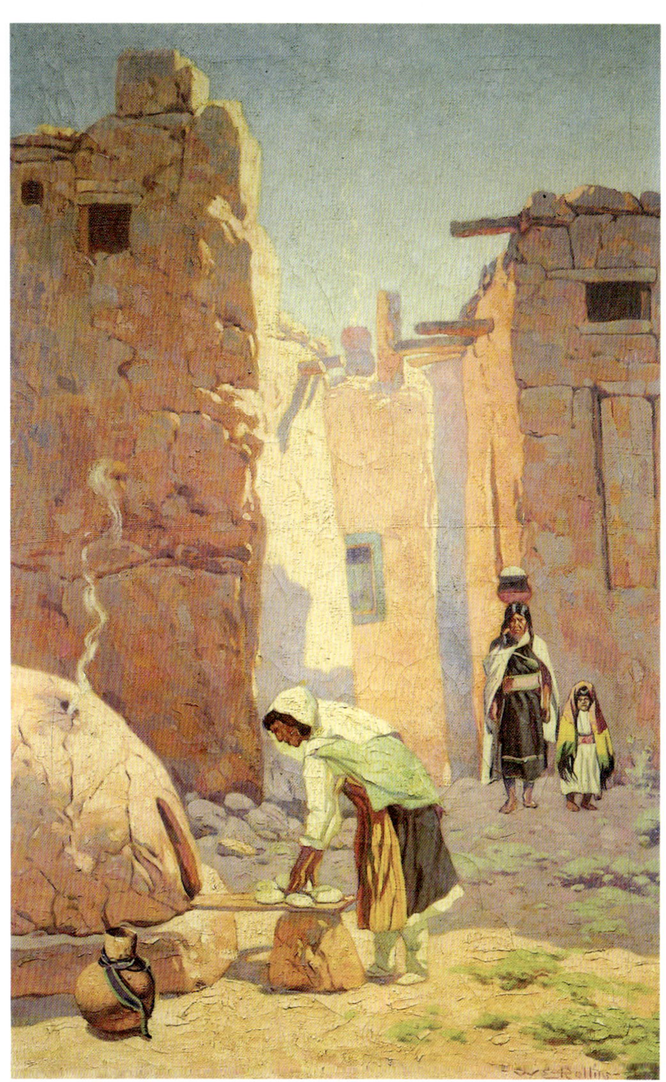

46. Warren Rollins, *The Thrall of the Past, Zuni Pueblo*, oil on canvas, 50 × 32 in.

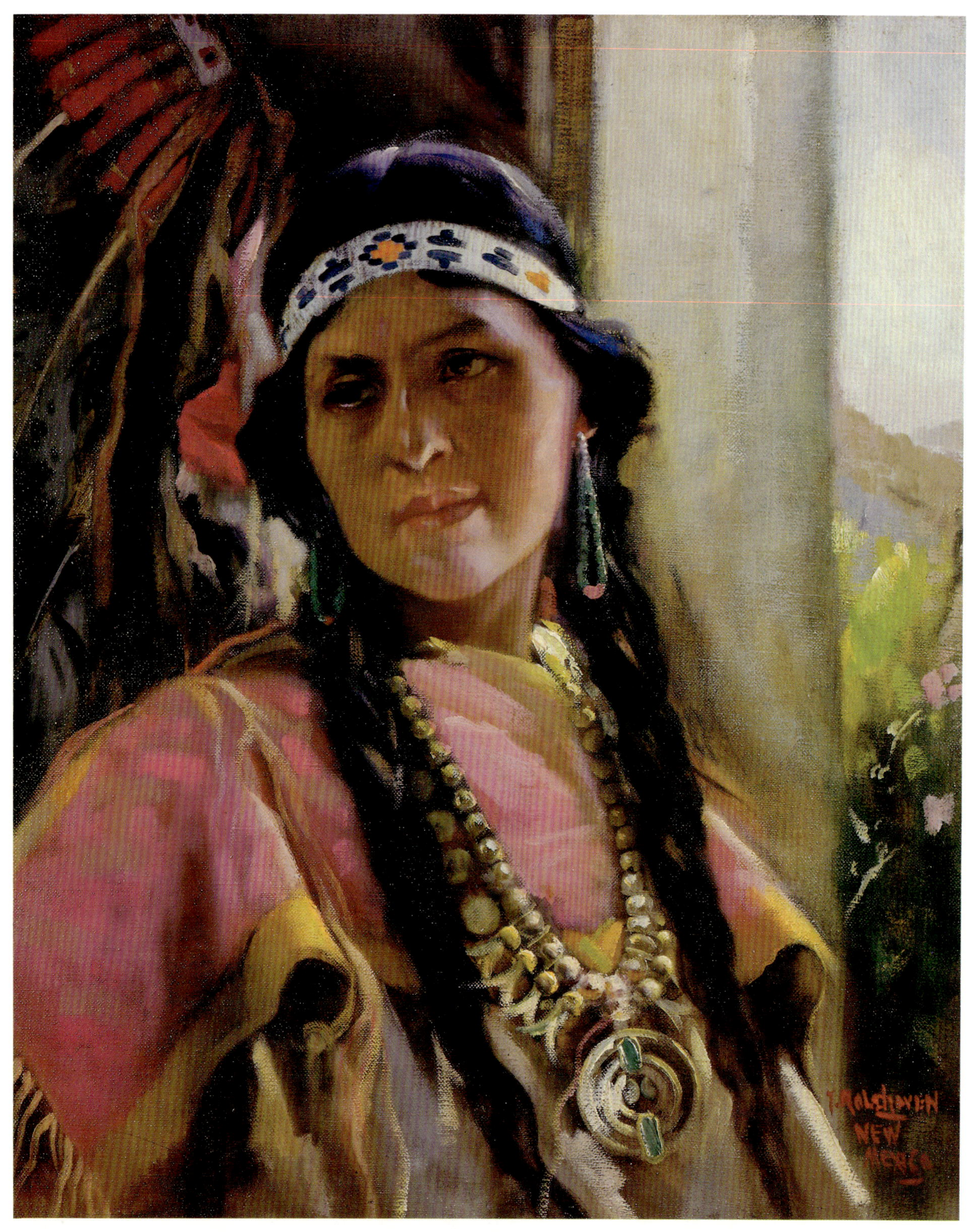

47. Julius Rolshoven, *Navajo Maiden,* oil on canvas, 24 × 20 in.

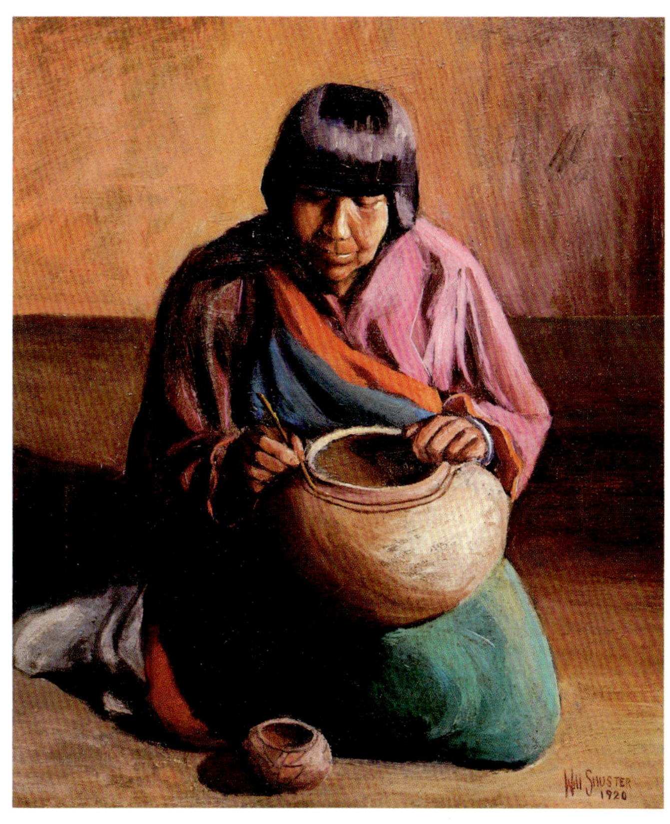

48. Will Shuster, *The Pottery Maker*, 1920, oil on canvas, 25-1/2 × 22 in.

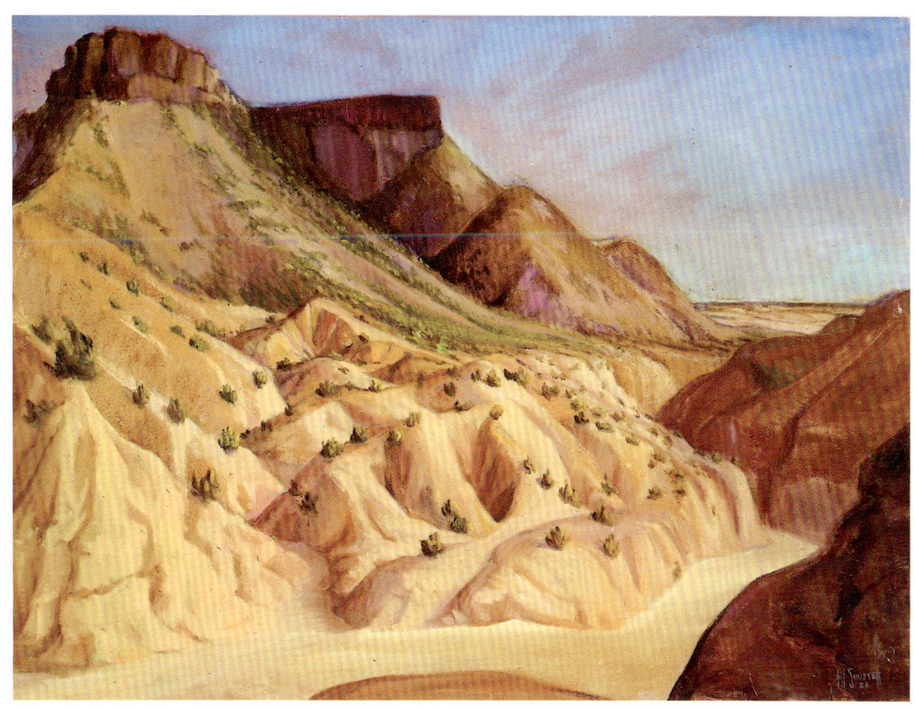

49. Will Shuster, *Formation on the Rio Grande,* 1923, oil on canvas, 30 × 40 in.

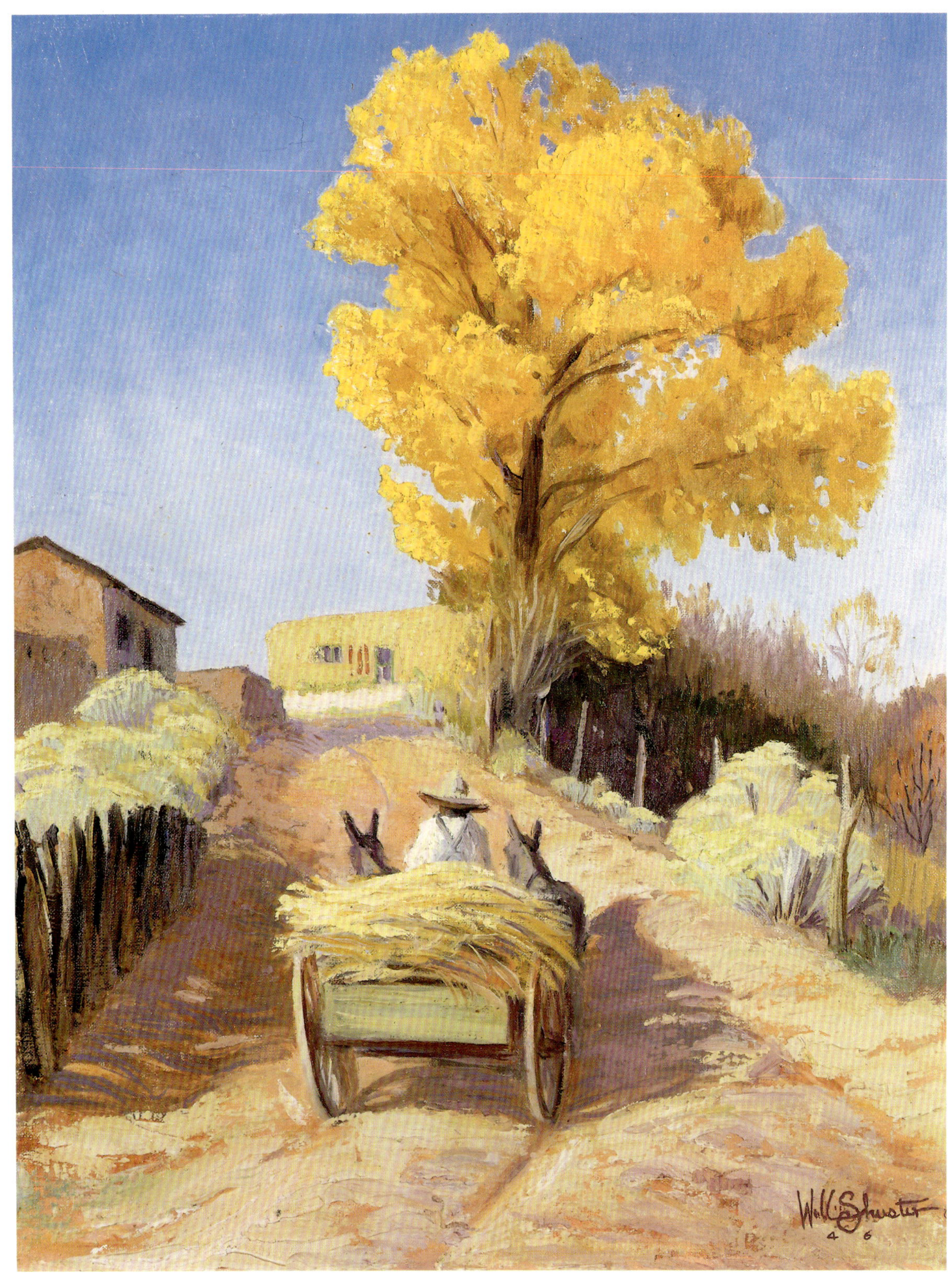

50. Will Shuster, *Cottonwoods, Tesuque,* 1946, oil on panel, 20 × 16 in.

70

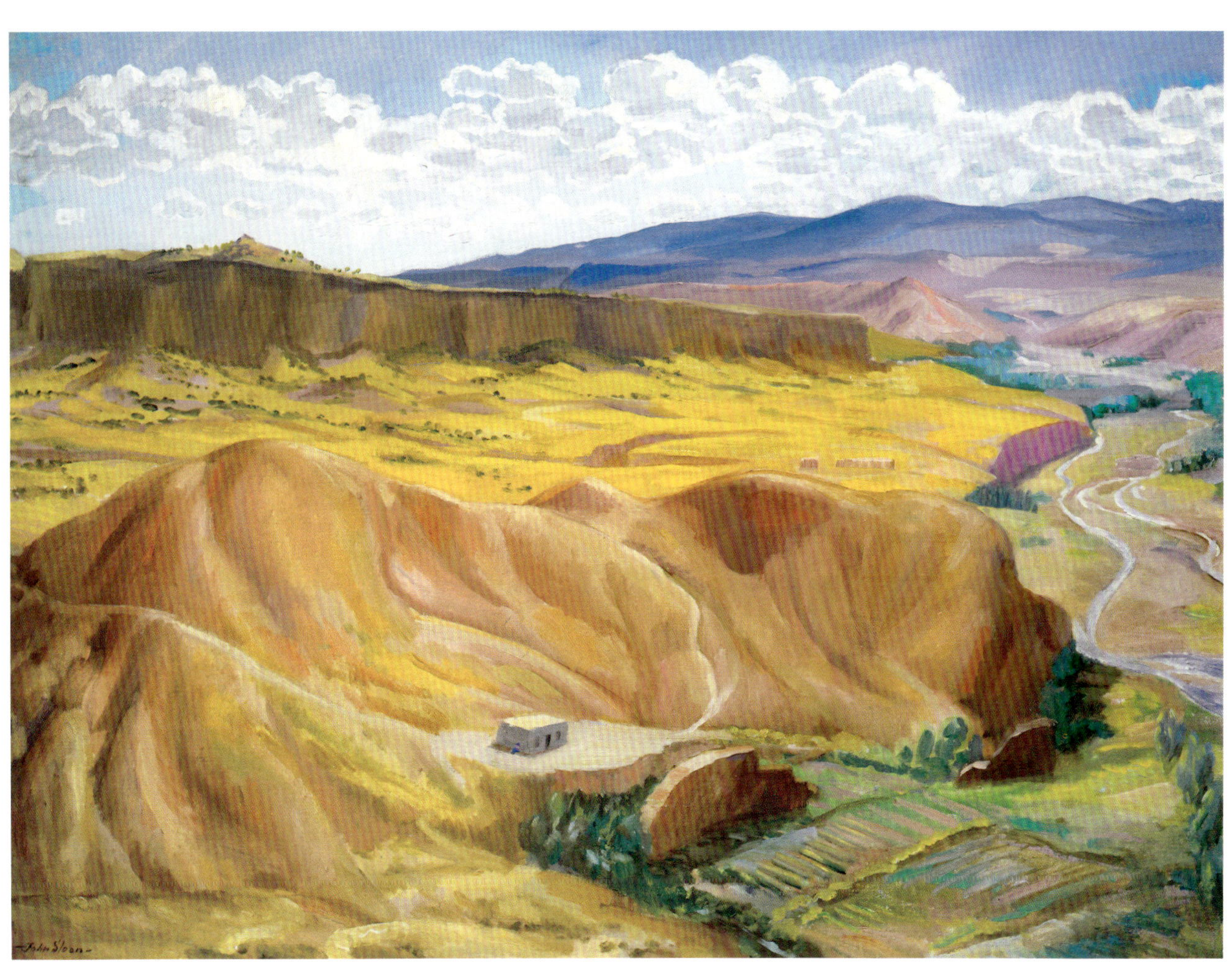

51. John Sloan, *Little Ranch House,* oil on canvas, 30 × 40 in.

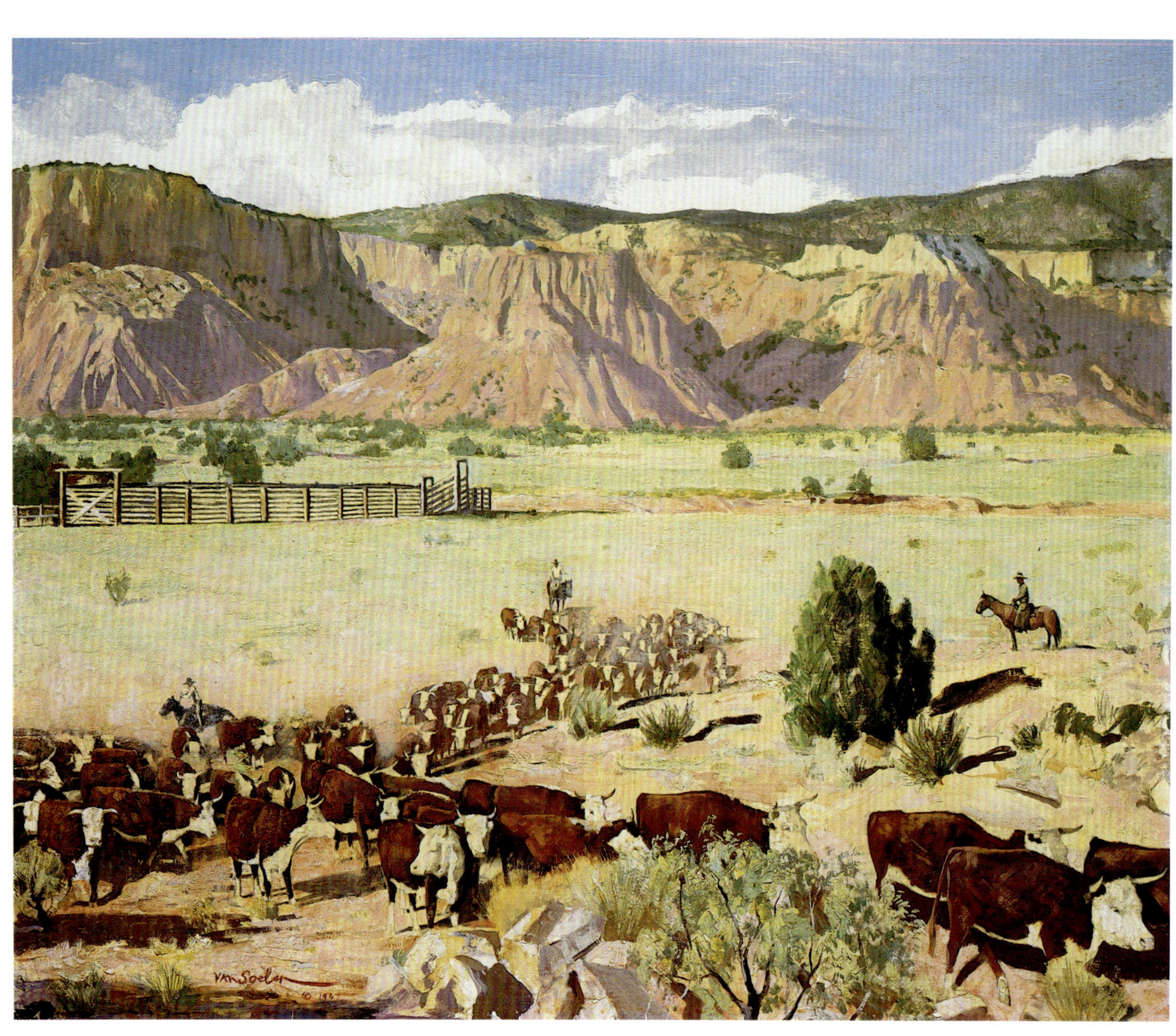

52. Theodore Van Soelen, *Grazing Cattle*, oil on canvas, 25 × 30-1/2 in.

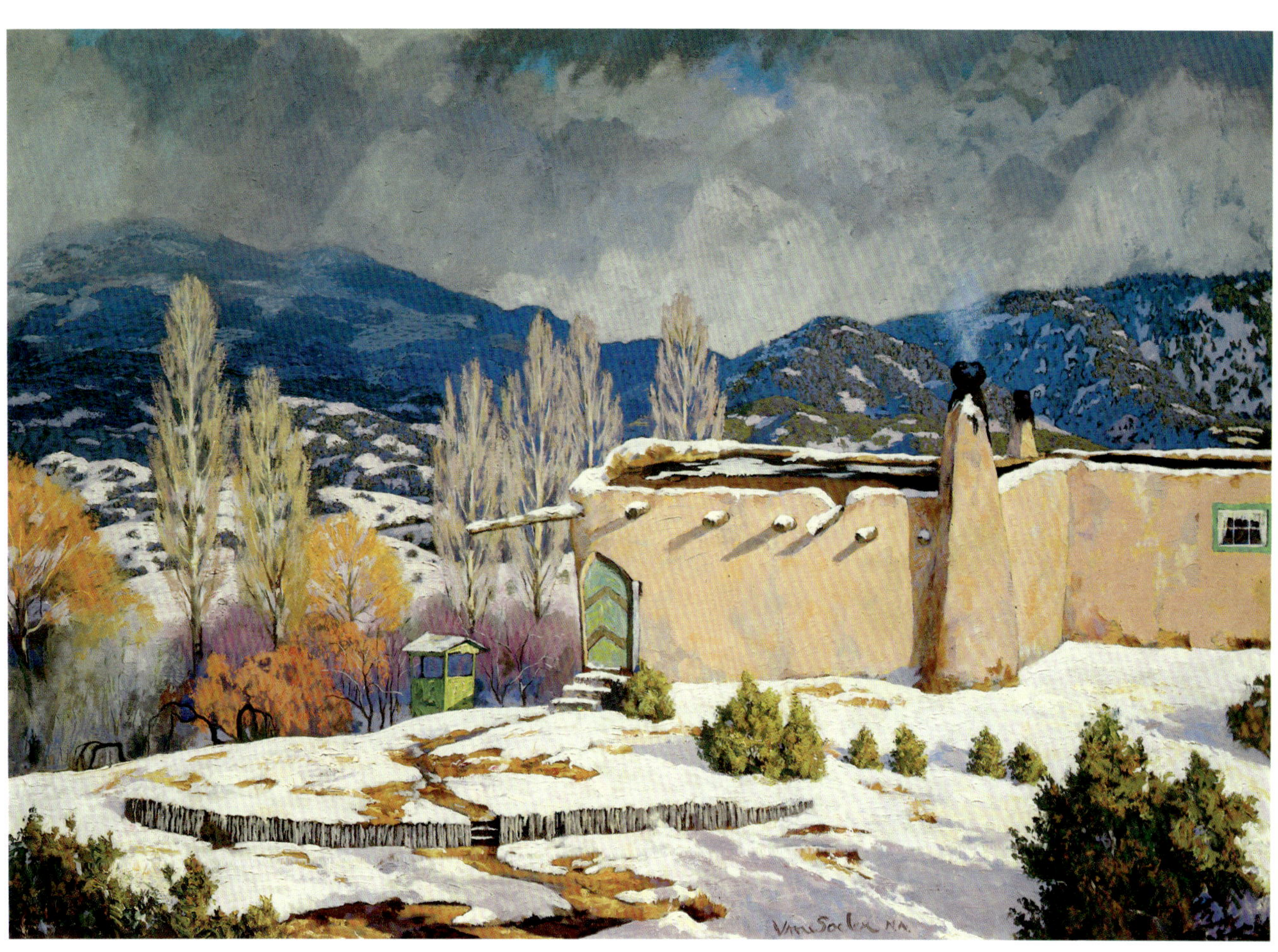

53. Theodore Van Soelen, *The Poet's [Witter Bynner] House,* oil on canvas, 33-1/2 × 47-3/8 in.

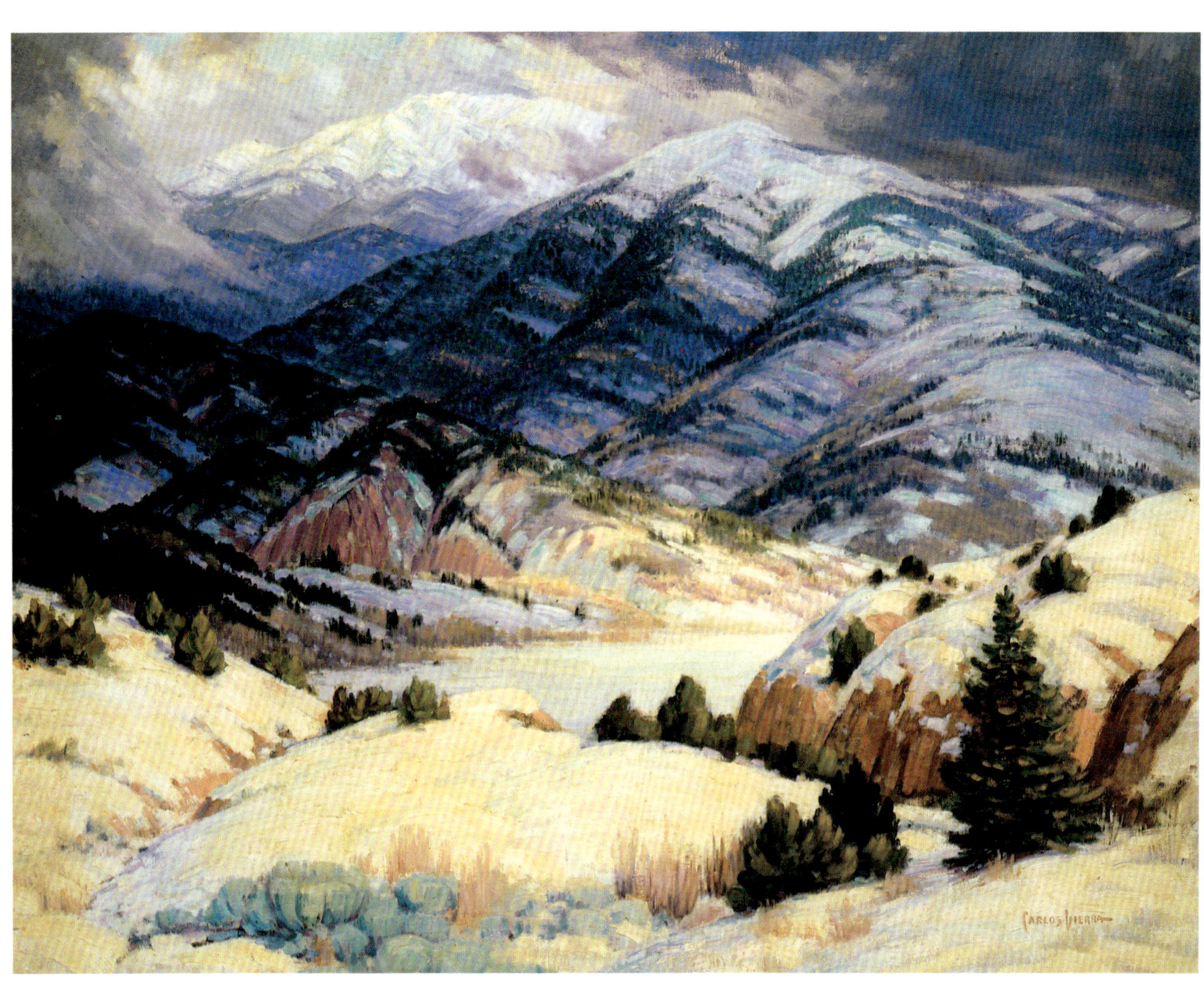

54. Carlos Vierra, *Northern New Mexico in Winter,* c. 1922, oil on canvas, 28 × 38 in.

74

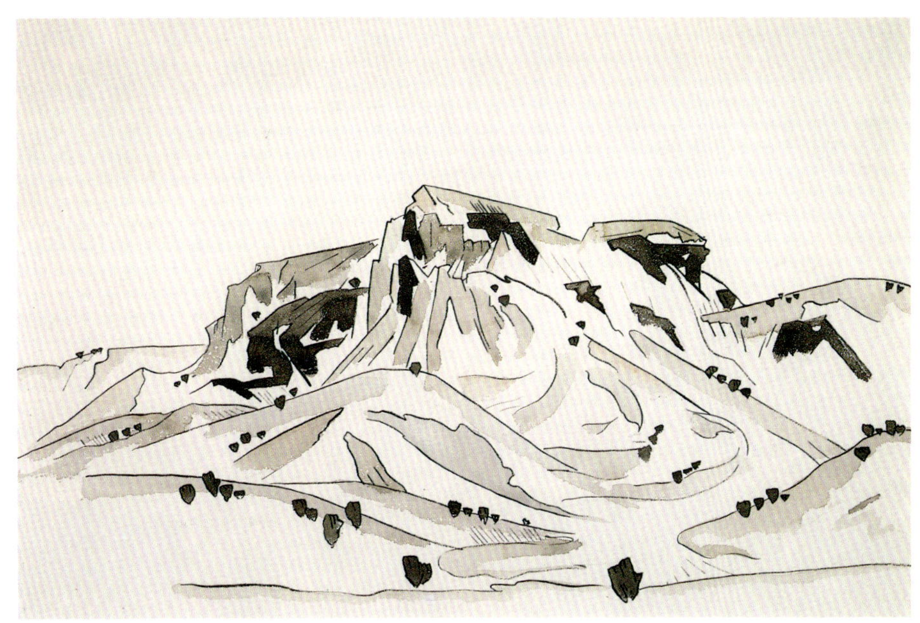

55. Cady Wells, *Black Mesa,*
watercolor, 14-1/4 × 21-1/2 in.

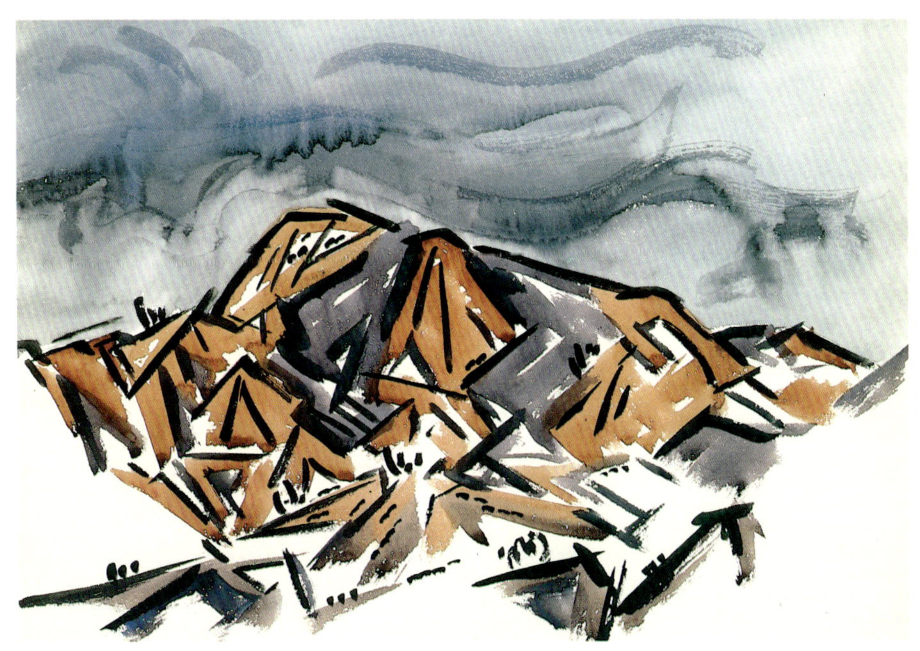

56. Cady Wells, *Mountain Peak
near Abiquiu, #53,* watercolor,
14-1/2 × 22 in.

Chronology, 1900–1942

1900 New capitol in Santa Fe, designed by firm of I. H. Rapp and W. M. Rapp, dedicated; remodeled 1951.
U.S. census reports population of New Mexico 195,310; Santa Fe 6,677.

1902 Sunmount Sanitorium, Santa Fe, established by Dr. Frank E. Mera; many influential Santa Feans later began New Mexico residence there, including Witter Bynner, Alice Corbin Henderson, John Gaw Meem, Carlos Vierra.

1904 Vierra becomes Santa Fe's first resident artist.

1907 School of American Archaeology founded by Edgar L. Hewett.

1908 The Eight stage legendary exhibition at Macbeth Gallery, New York; participants Robert Henri and John Sloan later visit New Mexico.

1909 Territorial legislature establishes Museum of New Mexico, which transforms old Palace of the Governors into combined historical museum and headquarters of the School of American Archaeology. Hewett serves as director of museum and school until his death in 1946.
Restoration of Palace of the Governors, Santa Fe, begins under supervision of Jesse Nusbaum; completed 1913.

c. 1910 Warren Rollins, who by 1893 was painting in Taos, holds art classes at Palace of the Governors.

1910 Stuart Davis studies with Henri until 1913.
Rollins exhibits at Palace of Governors.
U.S. census reports population of New Mexico 327,301; Santa Fe 6,589.

1912 Gerald Cassidy first visits Santa Fe.
Marsden Hartley travels to Paris, London, and Berlin through 1915; meets Wassily Kandinsky, Franz Marc, and other members of Blaue Reiter group.
New Mexico becomes forty-seventh state.

1913 Armory Show held in New York, Chicago, and Boston: first large-scale exposure of American audiences to advanced European art. Exhibitors include Paul Burlin, Andrew Dasburg, Randall Davey, and Homer Boss.
Burlin first visits Santa Fe; builds home there in 1914 and spends much time in New Mexico through 1920.
Sheldon Parsons settles in Santa Fe.
New Mexico Archaeological Society begins publishing *El Palacio,* Paul A. F. Walter editor.
Society for the Preservation of Spanish Antiquities in New Mexico founded.

1914 Parsons hired by Museum of New Mexico to act as art curator and director of exhibitions.
Olive Rush visits Santa Fe.

1915 William Penhallow Henderson completes murals commissioned by Frank Lloyd Wright for Midway Gardens, Chicago.
First official meeting of Taos Society of Artists (July), founded by O. E. Berninghaus, E. L. Blumenschein, E. I. Couse, W. Herbert Dunton, B. G. Phillips, and J. H. Sharp; annual meetings continue until 1927. First major TSA exhibition in Palace of the Governors, Santa Fe.
Willa Cather first visits New Mexico.
Panama-California Exposition held in San Diego, featuring a building devoted to Indian arts and an exhibition of Taos/Santa Fe paintings.

1916 Henri first visits Santa Fe; returns in 1917; spends six months in 1922; visits briefly in 1925.
Julius Rolshoven first visits New Mexico; remains two years.
Theodore Van Soelen moves to Albuquerque.
Alice Corbin and William Penhallow Henderson move to Santa Fe.

1917 Henry Balink first visits New Mexico; moves in 1923 to Santa Fe.
Leon Kroll first visits Santa Fe.
Museum of Fine Arts, Santa Fe, dedicated (November).
School of American Archaeology becomes School of American Research, with revised charter enabling it to collect Indian material.
Hewett commissions Indian artists Crescencio Martinez and Awa Tsireh to illustrate customs and ceremonies of Pueblo life. Studio space for

both, and for other Indian and Anglo artists, provided in Palace of the Governors.

Donald Beauregard begins murals in St. Francis Auditorium, Museum of New Mexico; Kenneth Chapman and Vierra later complete them.

1918 Gustave Baumann moves to Santa Fe.

Dasburg first visits Taos as guest of Mabel Dodge; establishes residence in 1933.

Hartley first visits Taos and Santa Fe; returns in 1919.

Encouraged by Henri, Hewett adopts open-door policy at Museum of Fine Arts, allowing any artist in the state to reserve exhibit space without going before a jury.

Nordfeldt and Henderson work as camouflage artists for U.S. Shipping Board, San Francisco.

TSA elects associate member Henri, honorary members Hewett and Frank Springer; Rolshoven made active member.

Mary Austin first visits Santa Fe; settles there in 1924.

Maria and Julian Martinez make first black-on-black pottery (San Ildefonso Pueblo).

1919 Davey first visits Santa Fe; settles there in 1920.

Fremont Ellis moves to Santa Fe from El Paso.

William Henderson builds studio on Camino del Monte Sol, Santa Fe.

Wladyslaw (Walter) Mruk moves to Santa Fe.

B. J. O. Nordfeldt moves to Santa Fe.

Rush establishes permanent home and studio in Santa Fe.

Sloan summers in Santa Fe; returns annually for thirty years.

Santa Fe Fiesta, established in 1712 and sporadically held thereafter, is revived by Hewett and others; includes Spanish Market.

Santa Fe Print Shop and gallery opens: Alice Corbin Henderson co-owner, Marsden Hartley first exhibitor.

1920 Jozef Bakos first visits Santa Fe; settles there in 1921.

Willard Nash moves to Santa Fe; leaves for California in 1936.

Will Shuster moves to Santa Fe.

Sloan sends group of Indian watercolors to Society of Independent Artists exhibition, New York. Austin arranges show at American Museum of Natural History, New York; includes Crescencio Martinez, Awa Tsireh, and others.

Poets Vachel Lindsay and Harriet Monroe visit Santa Fe; Carl Sandburg visits later in the 1920s.

Alice Corbin Henderson's *Red Earth: Poems of New Mexico* published.

Hartley's "Red Man Ceremonials: An American Plea for American Esthetics" appears in *Art and Archaeology* (January).

U.S. census reports population of New Mexico 360,350; Santa Fe 7,236.

1921 Los Cinco Pintores founded by Bakos, Ellis, Mruk, Nash, and Shuster. Group holds first exhibit as part of Santa Fe Fiesta at Museum of Fine Arts; dissolves 1926.

Davey teaches summer art classes at Kansas City Art Institute; returns there annually until 1924.

TSA elects associate members Sloan, Davey, and Nordfeldt.

New Mexico experiences drought and depression through 1923.

1922 Hartley's "The Scientific Esthetic of the Redman" appears in *Art and Archaeology* (March and September).

Raymond Jonson spends four months in Santa Fe; purchases land to build residence and studio; renews contact with Nordfeldt; returns in 1924; moves to Albuquerque in 1949.

Van Soelen moves to Santa Fe; later establishes permanent home in Tesuque.

Los Cinco Pintores exhibit as part of Santa Fe Fiesta in Museum of New Mexico; group exhibition travels through Midwest.

TSA elects associate members Birger Sandzen and Baumann.

Committee for the Preservation and Restoration of New Mexico Missions spearheaded by Anne Evans and Meem with support of Austin, Dan Kelly, Paul A. F. Walter, Frank Mera, and Vierra.

Indian Arts Association formed in Santa Fe to encourage native crafts.

Poet Witter Bynner arrives at Sunmount Sanitorium in Santa Fe.

1923   Davis summers in New Mexico.

Ellis exhibits pastels at Mariposa Shop.

Los Cinco Pintores hold exhibits and receptions in members' homes; announce plans to build their own cooperative gallery; exhibit together in Los Angeles.

New Mexico Painters group formed by Santa Fe artists Frank Applegate, Bakos, Baumann, William Henderson, and Nordfeldt and Taos artists Blumenschein, Victor Higgins, and Walter Ufer.

1924   Kenneth Adams joins Dasburg; shortly thereafter moves to Santa Fe.

Davey teaches portrait painting at Broadmoor Art Academy, Colorado Springs, in summer sessions; returns there annually through 1931.

William Henderson begins to practice architecture.

New Mexico Painters exhibit at Montross Gallery, New York; original members joined by Dasburg, Davey, Mruk, Sloan, and Van Soelen.

Austin settles in Santa Fe; in 1925 builds home, Casa Querida, on Camino del Monte Sol (today the Gerald Peters Gallery).

Spanish Colonial Arts Society created by Austin and Applegate.

1925   Homer Boss moves to Santa Fe.

William Henderson forms Pueblo-Spanish Building Company with partners; renovates and extends Sena Plaza as well as home of Misses Amelia and Martha White (later to become School of American Research). In 1926 he begins to design and produce handmade furniture.

Edward Hopper summers in Santa Fe.

Chappell School of Art, associated with Denver Art Museum, offers summer classes in Santa Fe; continues for two years.

1926   Jonson founds Atalaya Art School and conducts summer session; closes Fall 1927.

Nordfeldt has one-man show of etchings and wood-block prints at Smithsonian Institution, Washington, D.C.

A proposed summer culture program, a "Chautauqua," defeated by coalition of artists and writers.

Spanish and Indian Trading Post established in Santa Fe by Bynner, Dasburg, Mruk, Nordfeldt, and John Evans (son of Mabel Dodge Luhan).

Anglo artists first stage El Pasatiempo, a humorous parade intended to establish their presence in Santa Fe society.

Indian Detour excursions initiated to provide Santa Fe Railroad travelers a closer look at New Mexico scenic and historic sites.

Cyrus Baldridge first visits Santa Fe.

1927   Bakos, Dasburg, Jonson, Nash, Nordfeldt, and John E. Thompson (Denver artist and art teacher) form "Six Men"; exhibit at East-West Gallery, San Francisco.

Jonson acts as liaison between New Mexican artists and Museum of Fine Arts, Santa Fe, to organize "Modern Wing," in which thirty-two exhibitions are staged before the wing is discontinued in 1931.

TSA dissolved by members.

Willa Cather's *Death Comes for the Archbishop* published.

c. 1928   Willard Clark opens Santa Fe Plaza Art Gallery.

1928   Chappell School of Art cancels summer session; Santa Fe Art School formed by local artists and civic leaders to replace it.

Composer Aaron Copeland works in Santa Fe.

1929   Laboratory of Anthropology established in Santa Fe with grant from John D. Rockefeller; building designed by Meem completed in 1931.

E. Boyd arrives in New Mexico.

Spanish Colonial Arts Society purchases Santuario de Chimayo to prevent its dismantling.

Spanish Arts shop, sponsored by Spanish Colonial Arts Society, opens; closes 1934.

La Fonda hotel, Santa Fe, originally designed in 1920 by firm of I. H. Rapp, W. M. Rapp, and A. C. Hendrickson, remodeled and enlarged by Meem; Mary Elizabeth Jane Colter interior designer.

1930   Maynard Dixon and wife, Dorothea Lange, work in New Mexico and Arizona.

Gina Schnaufer first visits Santa Fe; returns in 1931 and marries Ernest Knee, spending most of 1930s there.

U.S. census reports population of New Mexico 423,317; Santa Fe 6,961.

1931   Exposition of Indian Tribal Arts, Grand Central Galleries, New York, is held, featuring southwestern Indian objects and including a publication with essays by Sloan, Oliver La Farge, Austin, Kenneth M. Chapman, Alice Corbin Henderson, and prominent anthropologists.

1932   At invitation of E. Boyd and Eugene Van Cleve, Cady Wells visits Santa Fe; studies two summers with Dasburg.

Dorothy Dunn teaches first studio classes at Santa Fe Indian School.

Brice Sewell appointed state director for Vocational Education and Training in New Mexico; utilizing city, state, and federal funds, he establishes statewide vocational centers to revive Hispanic craft traditions.

1933   Dasburg moves from Santa Fe to Taos.

Amelia White sponsors Gallery of American Indian Art (850 Lexington Avenue, New York), offering selected items from Exposition of Indian Tribal Arts (1931). Dolly Sloan manages gallery until 1937, when it closes and contents are distributed to museums on exposition tour.

Santa Fe/Rio Grande Painters formed, including E. Boyd and Gina Knee; dissolves 1936.

Museum of Modern Art exhibits "Painting and Sculpture from Sixteen American Cities;" includes Davey, Rush, Van Soelen.

Federal art patronage operates in New Mexico until 1943; includes four major New Deal art projects: Public Works of Art Project (PWAP, December 1933–June 1934, Jesse Nusbaum director, Gustave Baumann area coordinator); Treasury Section of Painting and Sculpture (October 1934–July 1939, Nusbaum director); Treasury Relief Art Project (TRAP, July 1935–June 1939, Nusbaum regional advisor and, with Emil Bisttram, local supervisor in New Mexico); and Works Progress Administration (WPA, August 1935–July 1943, R. Vernon Hunter director in New Mexico).

1934   Lloyd Moylan moves to Taos, later Santa Fe.

Native Market (nonprofit) operates as outlet for Hispanic crafts until 1940.

Baumann submits PWAP report on New Mexican federal art projects to Treasury Department, Washington, D.C.

1935   Nash included in "Abstract Art in America" exhibit, Whitney Museum of American Art, New York.

1937   Davey commissioned to paint murals, Will Rogers Shrine, Colorado Springs; hires Bakos as assistant.

Alice Corbin Henderson's *Brothers of Light: The Penitentes of the Southwest* published; illustrated by her husband, William P. Henderson.

Photographer Edward Weston works in Santa Fe area.

Arsuna School of Fine Arts opens in Mary Austin home; classes offered by Jonson and Alfred Morang, among others, in visual arts, music, and writing; School also operates gallery.

1938   Davey elected full Academician, National Academy of Design, New York.

Morang moves to Santa Fe.

Moylan paints WPA murals in New Mexico Normal University (now New Mexico Highlands University), Las Vegas, NM.

The Santa Fe Gallery opens in Sena Plaza.

Nine-member Transcendental Painting Group organized in Santa Fe; members include Jonson, Morang, William Lumpkins.

1939   Baumann publishes *Frijoles Canyon Pictographs,* illustrated with wood-block prints based on designs found at Frijoles Canyon, now part of Bandelier National Monument.

American Art Today exhibit at New York World's Fair includes work by Dasburg, Davey, Shuster, Baumann, Nordfeldt, Sloan, Gina Knee.

Transcendental Painting Group exhibits at Guggenheim Museum, Museum of New Mexico, and Golden Gate International Exposition, San Francisco.

c. 1941   Moylan becomes curator of Museum of Navajo Ceremonial Art, Santa Fe.

1942   Los Alamos selected national center for nuclear research.

❧ Artists' Biographies ❧

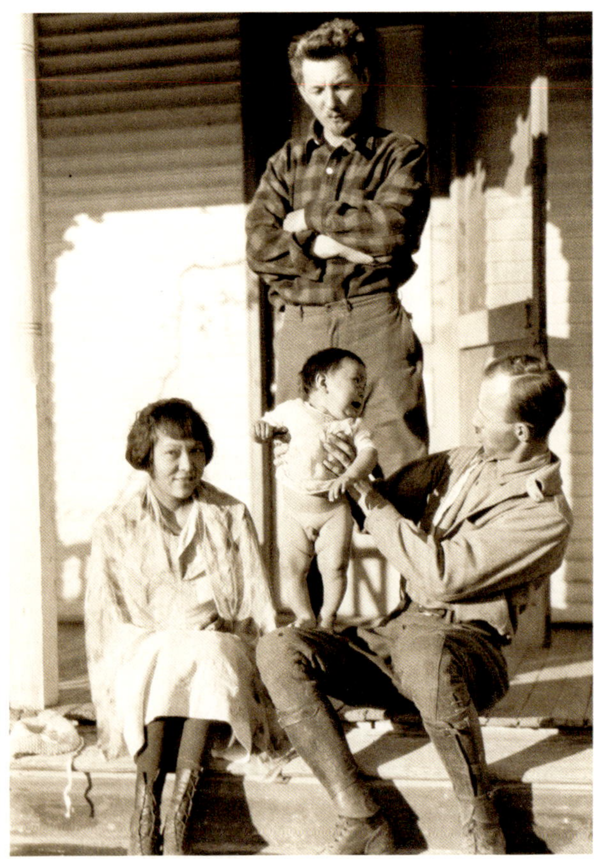

Jozef Bakos (standing), 1917

JOZEF G. BAKOS (1891–1977)

Bakos began his art education in his hometown of Buffalo at the Albright School of Art and continued it at the Toronto School of Art. He later studied privately with John E. Thompson in Buffalo, and in Denver. No longer a student, Bakos taught at the University of Colorado before visiting fellow artist Walter Mruk in Santa Fe in 1920. He was an active member of the art colony for over fifty years and helped form both Los Cinco Pintores (1921) and New Mexico Painters (1923). He was perhaps best known as a teacher, but he exhibited widely in major American museums, helping to increase national recognition and respect for New Mexico painting.

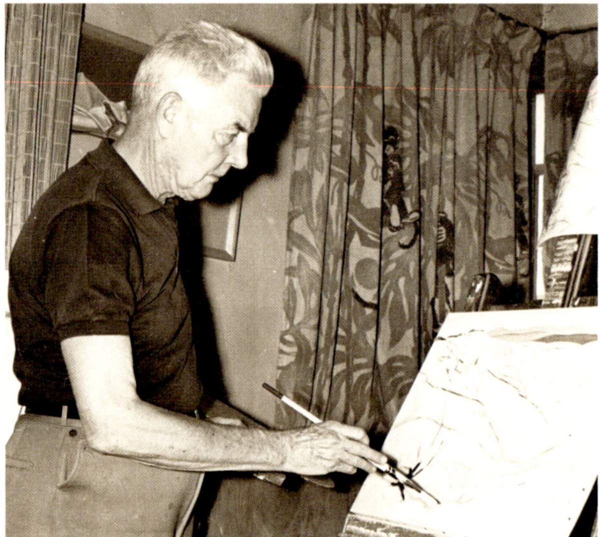

Cyrus Baldridge

CYRUS L. BALDRIDGE (1889–1975)

Before visiting Santa Fe in 1926, Baldridge had seen much of the world. From his birthplace in Alton, New York, his family moved frequently, yet Baldridge received art training from age ten, first studying with the famous newspaper illustrator Frank Holme. He graduated from the University of Chicago with a degree in English literature, took a job in commercial art, then worked as a field artist during World War I. After the war, he sketched in China, contributing drawings and articles to *Scribner's Magazine*. Baldridge and his wife traveled widely in the 1920s — to the Far East, Afghanistan, Persia, Africa — and the diverse and colorful cultures they encountered became inspiration for Baldridge's book illustrations. After 1932, Baldridge returned to the United States, where he continued to illustrate books and worked in film, designed stage sets, and wrote his autobiography. Frequent visits to the West in the 1920s, 30s, and 40s introduced southwestern themes to his art. In 1952, the Baldridges settled permanently in Santa Fe, where he worked two more decades, painting the desert and mountain country of New Mexico in watercolor and oil.

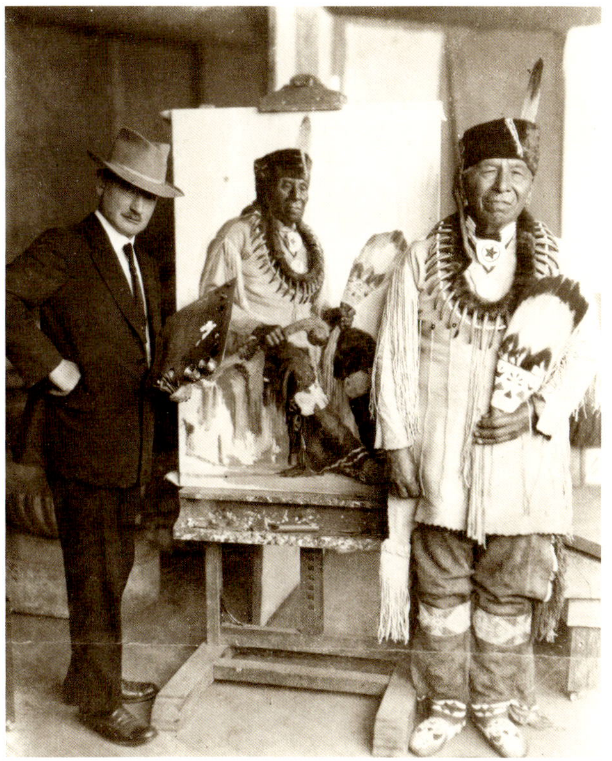

Henry Balink with son of Sitting Bull, Santa Fe

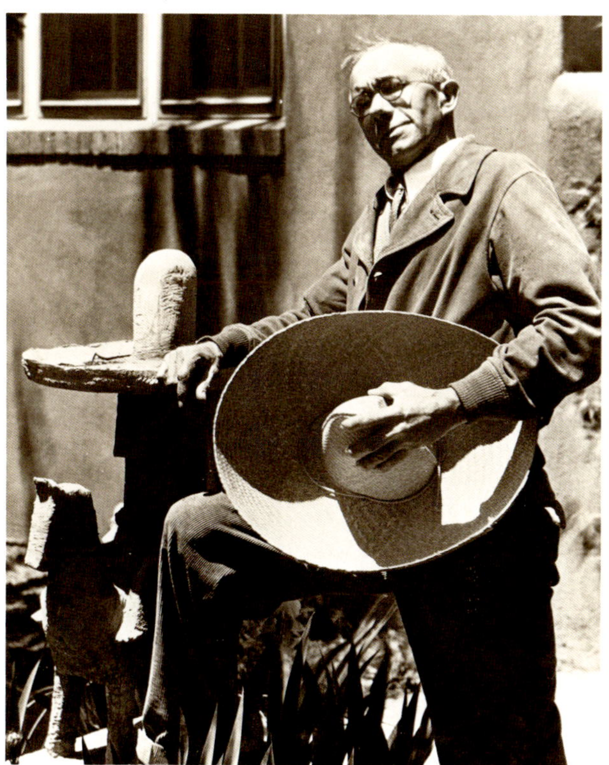

Gustave Baumann, Santa Fe, 1932

HENRY C. BALINK (1882–1963)

After five years of study at the Royal Academy in Amsterdam, Balink left his native Holland in 1914 for a visit to the United States. He returned to the United States in 1916, settling briefly in Chicago. Balink set out for New Mexico in 1917, inspired by a railroad travel poster. From Taos and Santa Fe he began to explore Indian country, eventually making portraits from some sixty-three tribal groups. Prized for their historical and ethnological values, Balink's Indian portraits, landscapes, and murals capture the character of a people and a way of life the artist saw changing quickly and irrevocably.

GUSTAVE BAUMANN (1881–1971)

Baumann was born in Magdeburg, Germany, but grew up in Chicago. He studied art in Munich and at the Art Institute of Chicago. In 1918 he and several other artists decided to see first hand the reputed clear air and light of New Mexico. Arriving first in Taos, Baumann soon chose to settle in Santa Fe. For over fifty years he participated actively in the art community — painting, making marionettes, experimenting with color woodblock prints, for which he became best known, and during the 1930s serving as the area coordinator of the Works Progress Administration (WPA).

HOMER BOSS (1882–1956)

Massachusetts-born Homer Boss participated quietly
in some of this century's most explosive art revolutions.
Study with William Merritt Chase, Thomas Anschutz,
and Robert Henri shaped the painter's early style; he
later exhibited in the 1910 Independents Show and the
epochal 1913 Armory Show. After teaching at the Independent School, Art Students League, and Parsons
School of Design in New York, Boss visited New Mexico in 1925 and, in 1933, settled permanently in Santa
Cruz. Always publicity shy, Boss's broadly executed realist portraits and landscapes speak eloquently of his
direct involvement with the Southwest.

PAUL BURLIN (1886–1969)

Most of Burlin's career was spent in New York, but he
spent much of the period from 1913 to 1920 in Santa
Fe. His early training as an illustrator was redirected
along more avant-garde paths when he encountered
the innovations of Robert Henri and Alfred Stieglitz.
Lured by romantic notions of the "primitivism" of the
Southwest, Burlin, soon after exhibiting in the Armory
Show, headed for New Mexico. Bold distortions of color
and form and natural patterning in the landscape char-
acterized Burlin's Santa Fe paintings. He introduced
fauve and expressionist modes to the art of New Mexico before returning to the East.

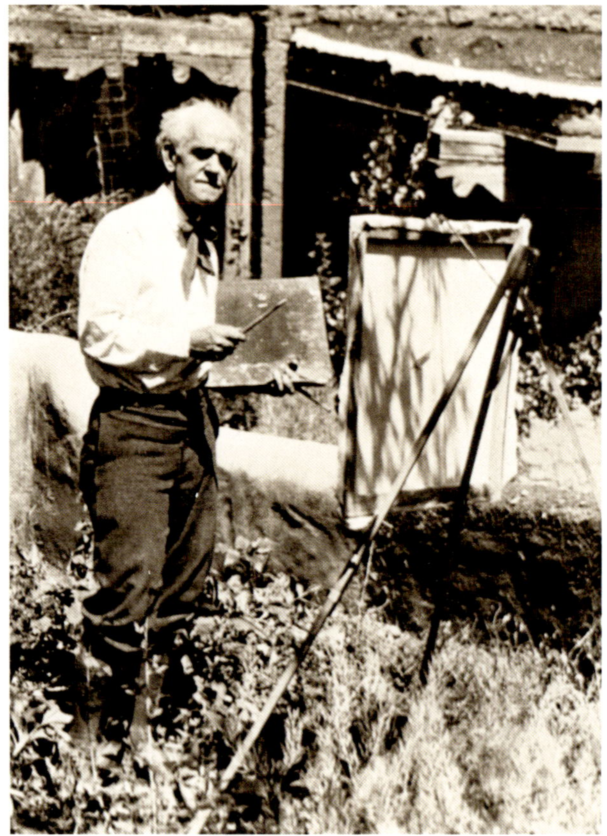

Gerald Cassidy, Santa Fe

GERALD CASSIDY (1879–1934)

Cassidy's brief formal art training included study in
Cincinnati with Frank Duveneck and at the Art Students League and the National Academy of Design in
New York. There he pursued a career in commercial art
and lithography. After a year spent painting in France,
Italy, Austria, and England, he settled in
Denver for a time. His declining health, however,
prompted a move to Albuquerque, where he began to
illustrate Indian subjects. He moved in 1912 to Santa
Fe and there met Edgar L. Hewett, founding director of
the Museum of New Mexico. Through Hewett, Cassidy
received his first mural commission, executed in 1915
at the Panama-California International Exposition in
San Diego. His many subsequent paintings of Indian
and desert life record a search for light and color
effects as well as an abiding love for the great open
spaces of the Southwest.

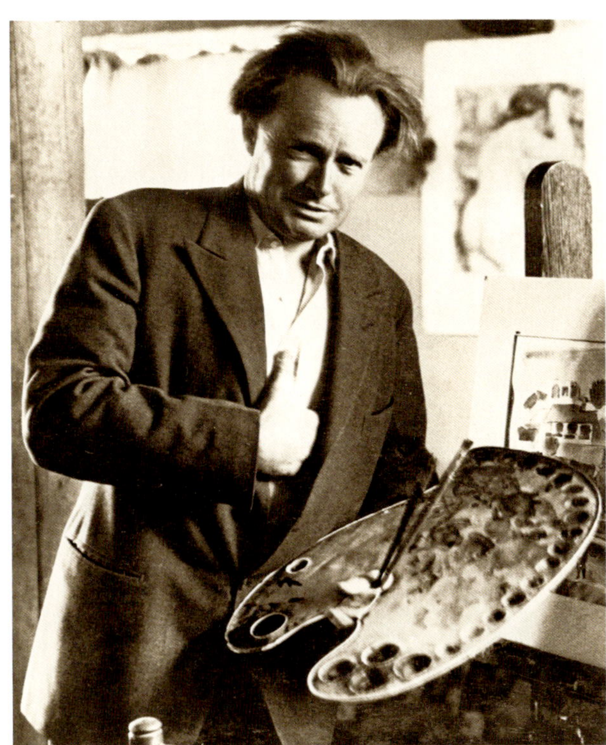

Andrew Dasburg, Santa Fe

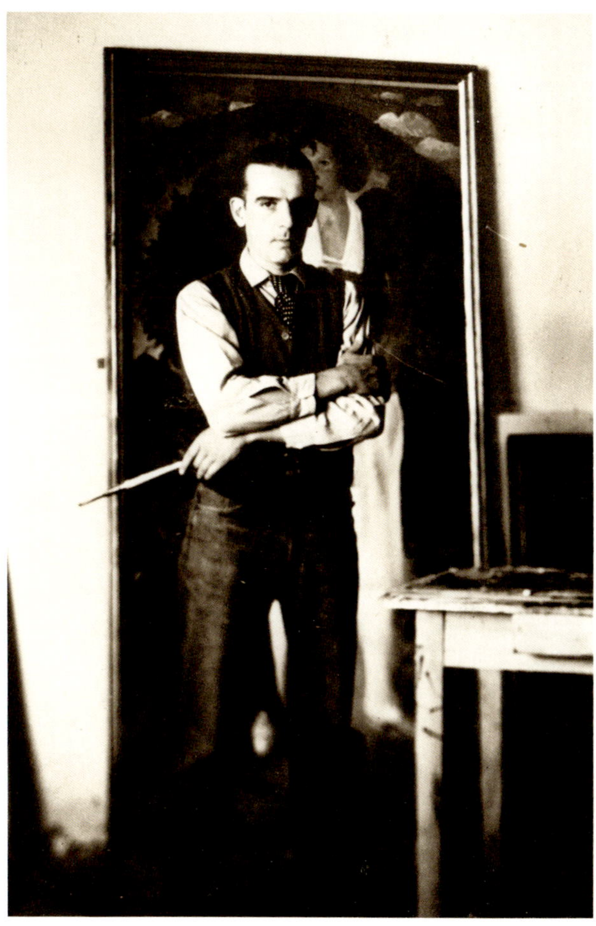

Randall Davey, Santa Fe

ANDREW DASBURG (1887–1979)

When Dasburg first visited New Mexico in 1918 at the invitation of Mabel Dodge, he was well acquainted with advanced art on both sides of the Atlantic. From his birthplace in Paris, Dasburg had been brought to New York at age five. He later studied at the Art Students League with Kenyon Cox and Birge Harrison, then with Robert Henri. He returned in 1909 to Paris, where he discovered Cézanne, whose art indelibly influenced his own. His modernist spirit is further suggested a few years later by his participation in the Gertrude Stein circle and in the radical Armory Show. After Dasburg's first New Mexico visit, he returned for several subsequent years to paint in the state. From 1921 to 1932 he lived in Santa Fe, building his own adobe home and sharing the colorful life of the artists' colony on Camino del Monte Sol. After 1933 he resided in Taos where, except during a period of illness between 1935 and 1945, his oils, watercolors, drawings, and pastels continued to evolve through several distinct periods of creativity.

RANDALL DAVEY (1887–1964)

A versatile realist in the modern spirit, Davey was the only one of Robert Henri's students to make Santa Fe his home. After a comfortable boyhood in East Orange, New Jersey, he studied architecture at Cornell University but then withdrew to paint. Among others committed to advanced art, he exhibited with the Independents and in the 1913 Armory Show. Eventually, Davey abandoned the working-class subjects favored by the Henri circle. He then turned to portraiture and — after his move to Santa Fe in 1919 — to landscape. Working in oils, encaustic, pastels, lithography, and etching, Davey blended Impressionist paint application with disciplined color and tonal analysis to create his figural pieces and the race-track scenes for which he became so well known.

Born in the wide-open mining town of Virginia City, Montana, Ellis traveled a good deal with his parents. A childhood visit to the Metropolitan Museum, where he was struck especially by Albert Bierstadt's work, convinced Ellis he wanted to paint. But practical considerations prevailed initially, and the young man studied optometry. His only formal art training came with a brief term at the Art Students League. Visiting Santa Fe from his home in El Paso in 1919, Ellis at age twenty-one decided to trade security for the uncertainties of a career spent interpreting Southwest landscape with a brush and paint. Once in Santa Fe, he and four friends founded Los Cinco Pintores. For sixty-five years Ellis recorded the landscape and people of New Mexico in rhythmic, light-charged canvases.

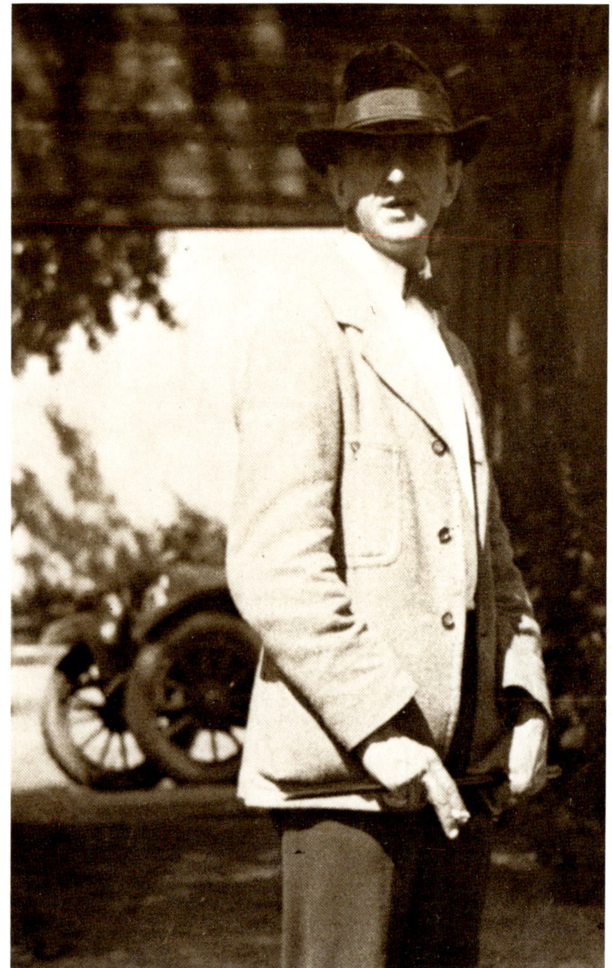

Marsden Hartley, Palace of the Governors,
Santa Fe, 1919

MARSDEN HARTLEY (1877–1943)

Hartley began and ended his career in Maine. Restlessly on the move his entire life, he spent much of 1918 and 1919 in the Southwest. Like many who visited New Mexico, Hartley came at the invitation of Mabel Dodge in Taos, although he soon moved to Santa Fe. Hartley's New Mexico work is startling in its variety and includes vivid but serene still lifes and undulating expressive landscapes. Acknowledged now as an American master, his original and highly expressionist work bears the imprint of a complex personality that produced some of the most intense images of New Mexico that exist.

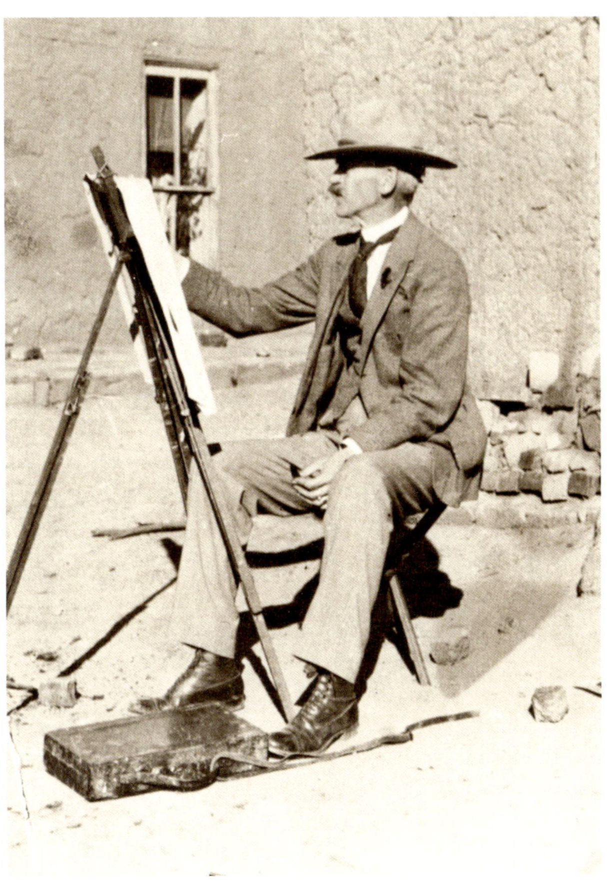

William Penhallow Henderson

WILLIAM PENHALLOW HENDERSON (1877–1943)

After a boyhood spent in Massachusetts, on a Texas cattle ranch, and in a small Kansas town, Henderson studied art in Boston with Edmund C. Tarbel. A three-year traveling scholarship from the Boston Museum of Fine Arts in 1901 enabled him to study abroad and to see much of Europe. He subsequently painted, illustrated, and taught in Chicago before moving in 1916 to Santa Fe. Henderson, until his death in 1943, was an active mural painter, architect, and furniture designer, incorporating Indian and Hispanic themes and images into his work. Appointed to a federal arts project, he completed easel paintings and six murals for the Santa Fe Federal Court Building. His work is immediately recognizable for its high-keyed, emotive color and expressive form.

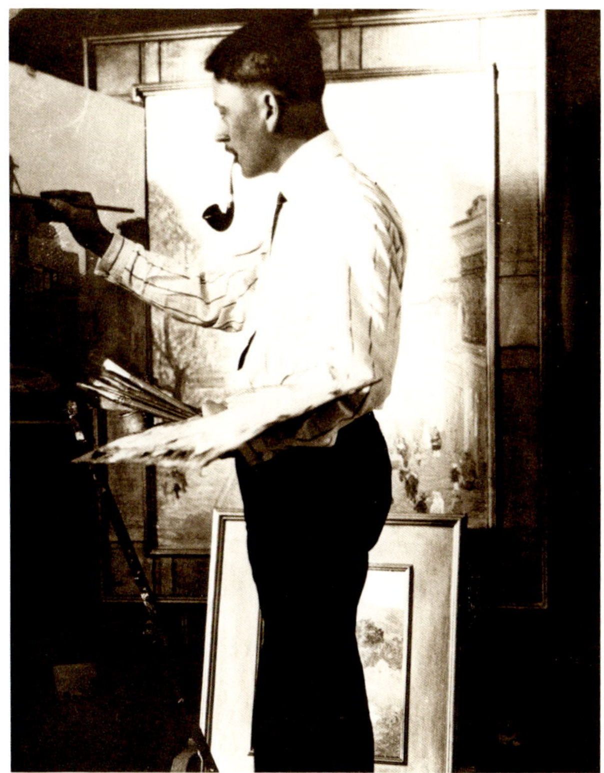

Robert Henri

ROBERT HENRI (1865–1929)

Henri spent time in Santa Fe in 1916, 1917, 1922, and 1925. During that time, he produced some thirty portraits, mainly of Hispanic and Indian subjects. His enthusiasm for New Mexico brought a number of artists to the area, including John Sloan and George Bellows. Henri crusaded actively against academic conservatism, enlisting younger artists (such as Sloan) and his students (Bellows, Edward Hopper, Morgan Russell, and Stuart Davis) in the cause of artistic freedom and unflinching realism, a belief that led his detractors to dub Henri's group the "Ashcan" school. In 1908 Henri and other members of the Ashcan "Eight" achieved notoriety with their exhibit at Macbeth Gallery in New York. When Henri met Dr. Edgar Hewett of Santa Fe's School of American Archaeology in 1914, the museum director urged Henri to paint in New Mexico. Henri's strong personality and liberal ideas regarding museum policy, particularly unjuried exhibitions, left a lasting imprint on the newly opened Museum of New Mexico.

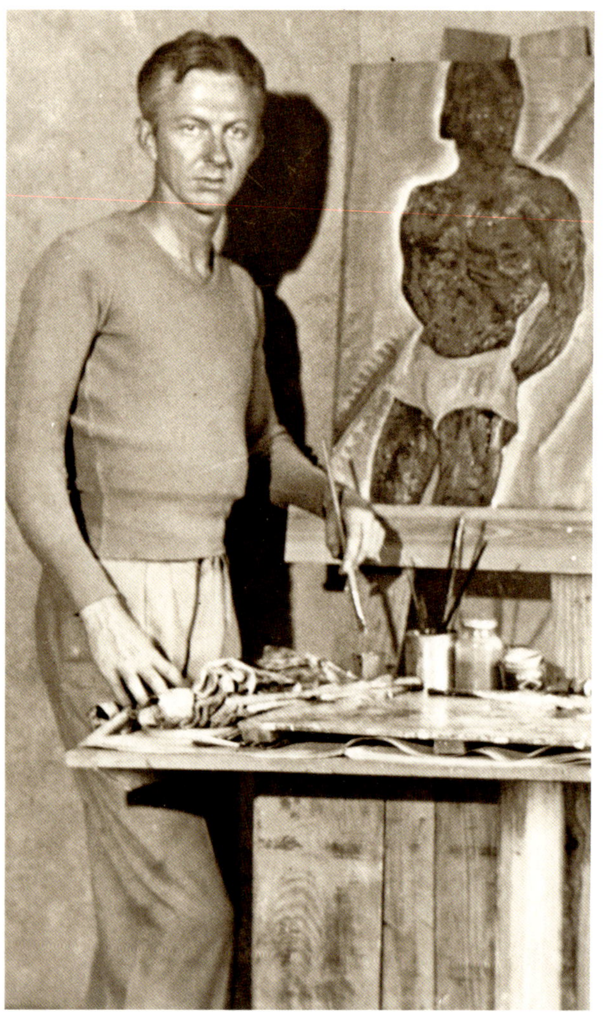

Russel Vernon Hunter, Texico, 1930–1932

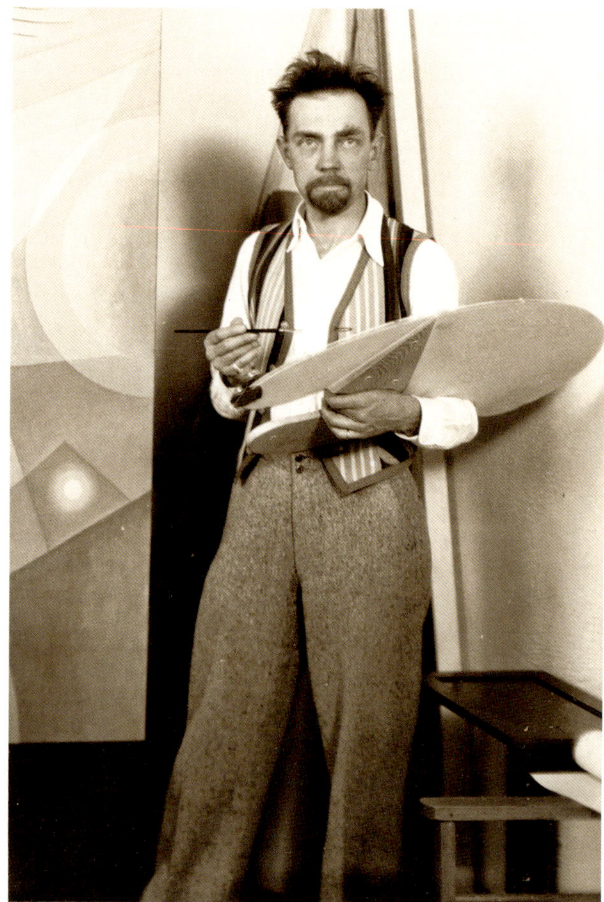

Raymond Jonson, c. 1935

RUSSEL VERNON HUNTER (1900–1955)

Illinois-born Hunter studied at the Art Institute of Chicago and with Stanton MacDonald-Wright in Los Angeles. He worked as a designer and teacher before joining the Works Progress Administration (WPA), serving as state director for New Mexico from 1935 to 1942. Under Hunter's supervision the WPA published *Portfolio of Spanish Colonial Design in New Mexico*. He later held administrative positions in the arts at the Dallas, Texas, and Roswell, New Mexico, museums. He painted in a vigorous, realist manner, which can be seen in murals executed in Texas, New Mexico, and Michigan.

RAYMOND JONSON (1891–1982)

Jonson, who became a champion of modern art in the Southwest, studied at the Portland (Oregon) Art Museum, the Chicago Academy of Fine Arts, and the Art Institute of Chicago before he was twenty. He moved in 1924 to Santa Fe, where his painting took a decisive turn toward the abstract. Discovering rhythmic structure inherent in the landscape, Jonson increasingly painted the essence of a subject rather than its details, until he achieved what he termed "absolute" painting. Respected as a teacher, Jonson was appointed to the art faculty of the University of New Mexico in 1934; he moved to Albuquerque in 1949. In the university art gallery named in his honor, Jonson organized more than three hundred exhibitions between its opening in 1950 and his death in 1982.

86

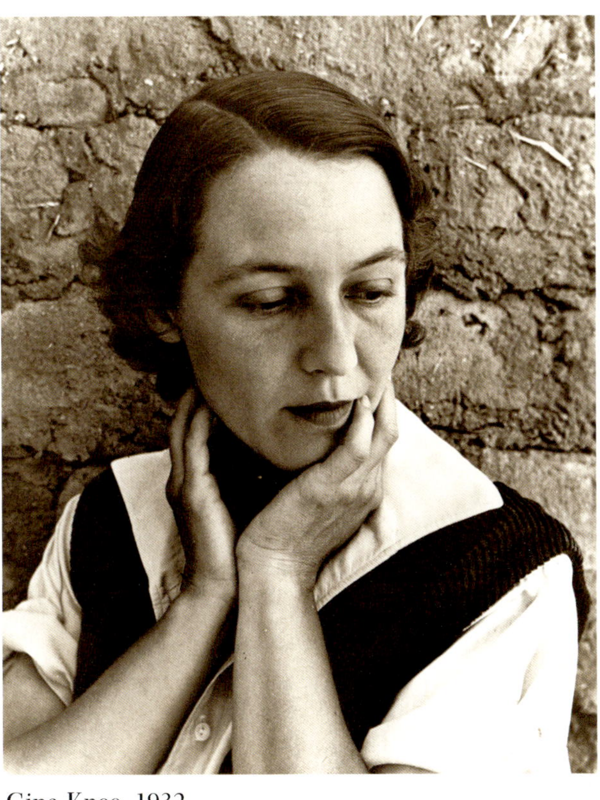

Gina Knee, 1932

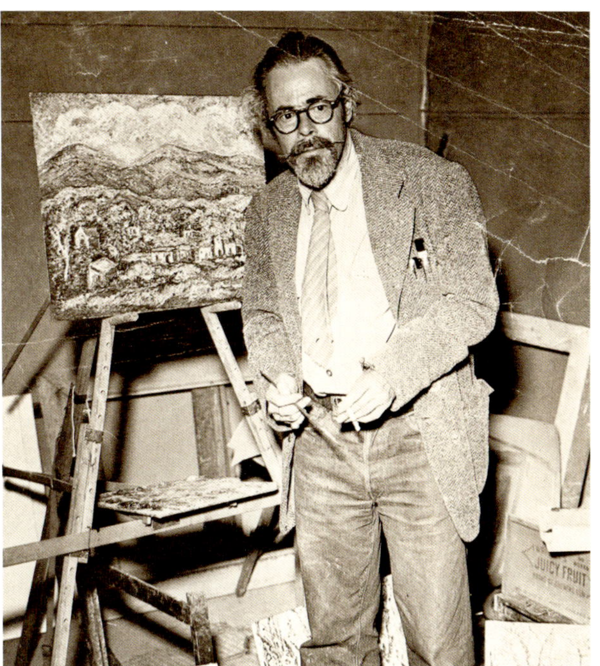

Alfred Morang

GINA SCHNAUFER KNEE (1898–1982)

Born in Ohio, Knee studied briefly at the Art Students League and for a summer with Ward Lockwood. In New Mexico, where she settled in 1930, the landscape was her primary subject. Abstracting from natural forms, she used a modernist vocabulary to describe the underlying forms and forces in nature. She exhibited with the Rio Grande Painters in the mid-1930s, and her watercolors, influenced by John Marin's work, were widely collected in the Southwest. Married in 1945 to painter Alexander Brook, Knee continued to paint, illustrate, and teach, first in Georgia and then at Sag Harbor, New York.

ALFRED G. MORANG (1901–1958)

As a child in Maine, Morang's formal schooling was hampered by his delicate health. He was taken out of school in the sixth grade to be tutored privately and receive violin instruction. At age sixteen, Morang developed an interest in art; he studied with artists who summered near his home and then with Impressionist Carrol S. Tyson and landscapist Henry B. Snell. Morang's music and art studies continued in Boston during the 1920s. After his marriage to fellow music student Dorothy Clark, the couple settled in Portland, Maine, where both gave music lessons and painted. With the encouragement of his friend Erskine Caldwell, Morang began to write and in the 1930s published a number of short stories. Morang was later diagnosed as tubercular, and he and his wife moved to Santa Fe in 1938. Although he maintained his interests in music and writing, Morang turned more decisively to painting. He taught at the Arsuna School of Fine Arts, participated in WPA art projects, and applied his Impressionist painting style to the qualities of light and atmosphere he found in Santa Fe. A tragic studio fire ended Morang's life in 1958.

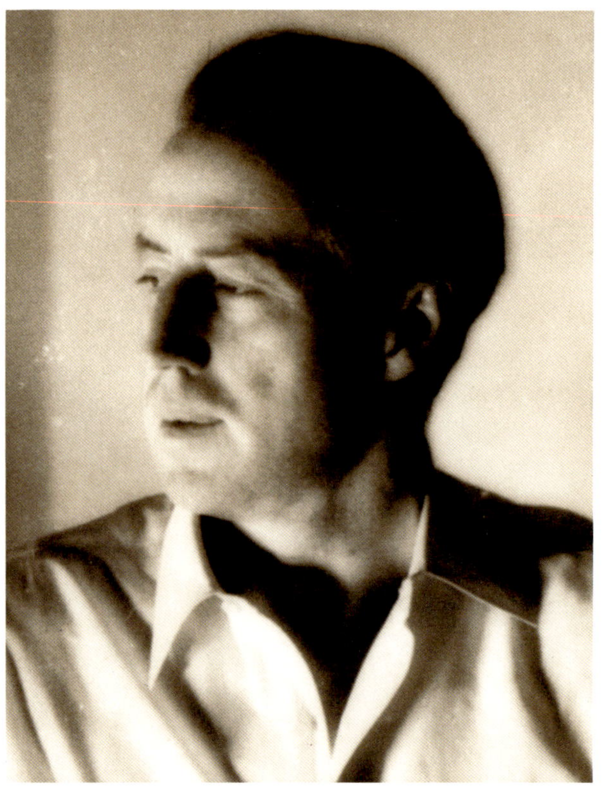

Lloyd Moylan

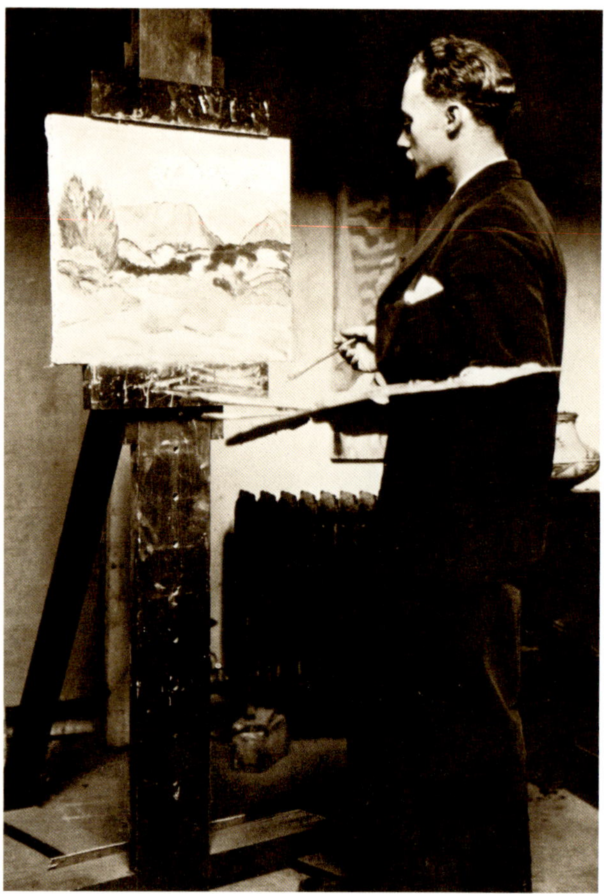

Willard Nash, Palace of the Governors, Santa Fe, 1921

LLOYD MOYLAN (1893–1963)

A versatile painter and printmaker, Moylan first trained in his hometown at the Minneapolis Art Institute, then at the Art Students League from 1917 to 1919. A teaching position at the Broadmoor Art Academy in Colorado Springs brought him west. Trips to Mexico exposed Moylan to the burgeoning mural movement there and inspired him to execute several mural commissions in the Colorado Springs area. Eventually, investigating Indian themes for his work, Moylan gravitated to New Mexico, where his mural work continued in 1938 under WPA sponsorship. His oils, watercolors, and lithographs emphasize line and pattern in a semi-abstract manner.

WILLARD NASH (1898–1943)

"I am an experimenter in art," declared Willard Nash in 1935, "and have worked through many phases, going step by step deeper into the mysteries of esthetics." Nash's artistic journey began as a student in Detroit and took him to Santa Fe in 1920 in search of a stimulating environment. When he began to study with Andrew Dasburg, Nash encountered the work of Cézanne, whose rigorously structured paintings began to influence his own New Mexico landscapes. A founding member of Los Cinco Pintores, Nash built a home and studio alongside his colleagues' on Camino del Monte Sol. In 1936 he left Santa Fe for teaching positions in California.

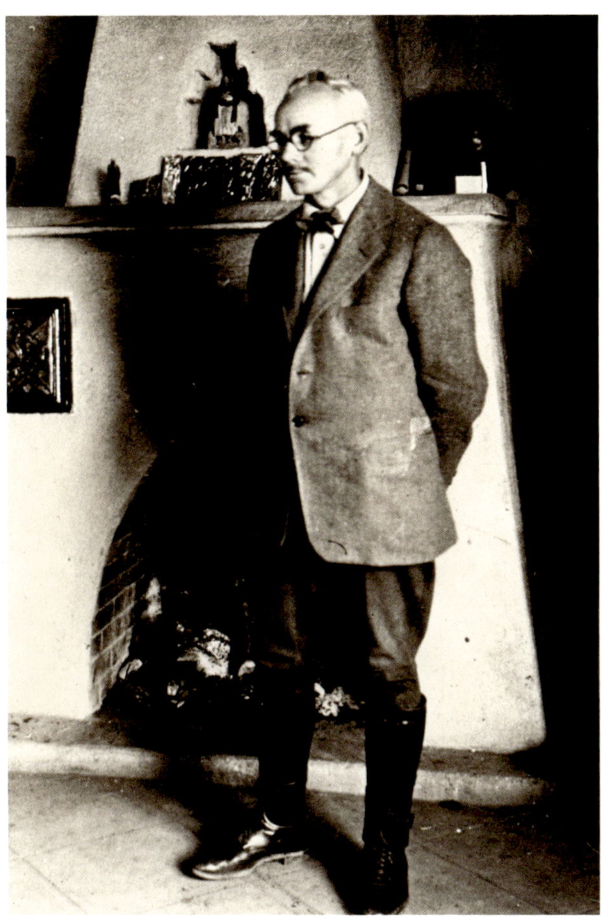

B. J. O. Nordfeldt

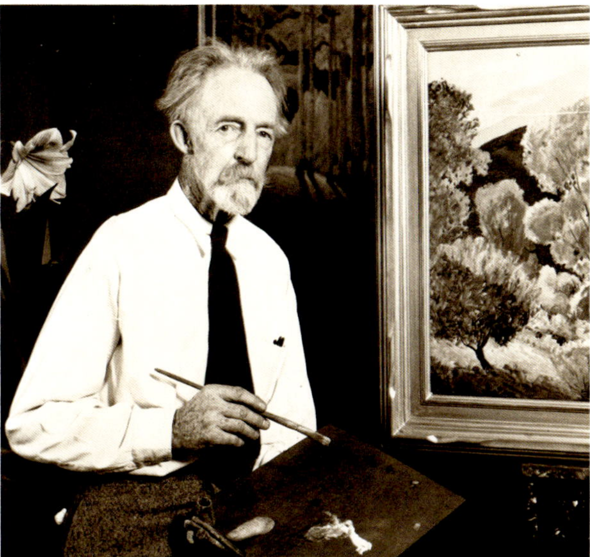

Sheldon Parsons, Santa Fe, c. 1935

B. J. O. NORDFELDT (1878–1955)

Nordfeldt emigrated to Chicago in 1891 from his native Sweden. After a year of training at the Art Institute of Chicago, he began a decade of further art studies, painting, and printmaking. In 1919 he established residence in Santa Fe, where he lived for the next twenty years. In his paintings, etchings, and lithographs he analyzed the rugged southwestern landscape or expressed fascination with his Hispanic neighbors. Elements of Cézanne and the Fauves are present in his work, along with a personal strain of expressionism. From 1934 to 1937 Nordfeldt divided his time among Wichita, Minneapolis, and Santa Fe, where he taught, painted portraits, and made lithographs for the PWAP. In 1937 he moved to Lambertville, New Jersey, which became his home for the rest of his life.

SHELDON PARSONS (1866–1943)

President McKinley and Susan B. Anthony were two of the famous Americans whose portraits Sheldon Parsons painted in the early 1900s. His talent for portraiture had emerged while he was still a student at the National Academy of Design, and a successful career in New York seemed assured. But his wife's death in 1913 abruptly changed his plans. The artist and his young daughter sold all their possessions and took the train west to Denver. There Parsons suffered a relapse of tuberculosis and was advised by doctors to try New Mexico's climate. When well enough to travel, Parsons and twelve-year-old Sara boarded a southbound train. In Santa Fe they were welcomed into the community by helpful citizens willing to exchange the necessities of life for Parsons's paintings. As the artist recovered his health he began painting landscapes — a longstanding interest of his. Absorbed with the color and light of his new environment, he recorded the town, nearby Indian pueblos, and the imposing New Mexico desert and mountains. In time Parsons became a well-known artist, accommodating his early Barbizon and Impressionist training to the light-drenched scenes of the Southwest. He served as an early administrator at the Museum of New Mexico, assisting in that capacity many later arrivals to the artistic community.

WARREN E. ROLLINS (1861–1962)

Though he eventually became known as "the dean of the Santa Fe art colony," it was as an itinerant sign painter that Rollins first came to know the West. He trained at the San Francisco Art Association School of Design and served briefly as its assistant director, leaving to satisfy his intense curiosity and interest in the American Indian. With his wife and family Rollins traveled the vast, isolated spaces of the West, searching for Indian material. His wanderings led from California and Oregon to the Dakotas, then through New Mexico and Arizona. By 1893 Rollins was painting in Taos, but he continued to explore the back country, often in the employ of the Santa Fe Railway. Favorite painting sites were Chaco Canyon, Zuni (where he spent nearly two years), and among Arizona's Hopi and Navajo. Rollins studied ardently the Navajo and Hopi ceremonies and made numerous sketches, which he later developed into large studio pieces or murals for public and private buildings in New Mexico. He established a permanent home in Santa Fe, taught painting classes at the Palace of the Governors, and served as the first president of the Santa Fe Arts Club.

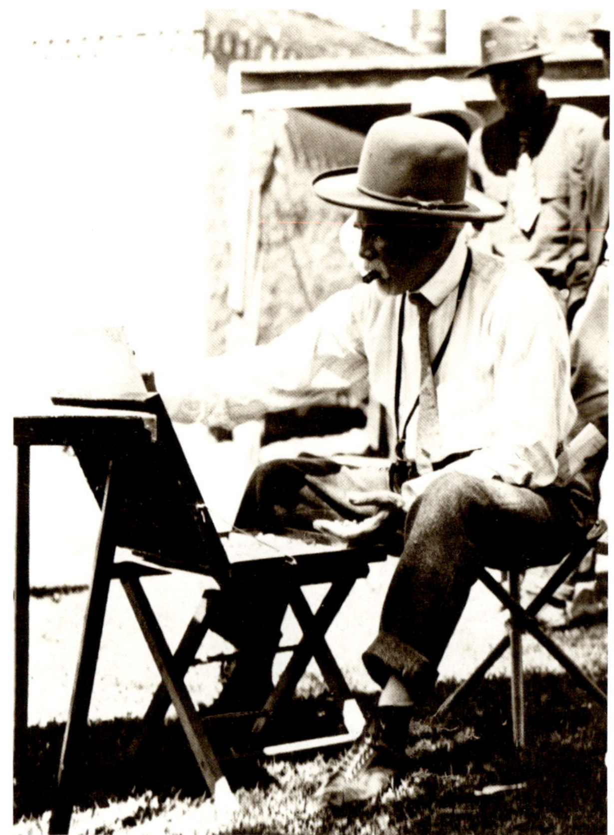

Julius Rolshoven, Palace of the Governors patio, Santa Fe Fiesta, Santa Fe, 1919

JULIUS ROLSHOVEN (1858–1930)

Rolshoven, who spent forty years as an American expatriate in Italy, relied on diverse environments for his stimulation. An ancient Florentine castle served as his studio and principal residence from 1907 until his death in 1930, but he frequently summered in Santa Fe and Taos during those years. Rolshoven was born in Detroit and studied art in New York, Dusseldorf, Munich, and Paris. He was especially influenced by his mentor, Frank Duveneck. A wedding trip to the Southwest in 1916 so captivated the artist that he stayed two years in New Mexico before returning to Florence. While in Santa Fe, Rolshoven developed a warm friendship with Museum of New Mexico Director Edgar L. Hewett, who invited him to exhibit in the museum's dedication show. A Rolshoven Indian portrait remained in the newly established permanent collection.

90

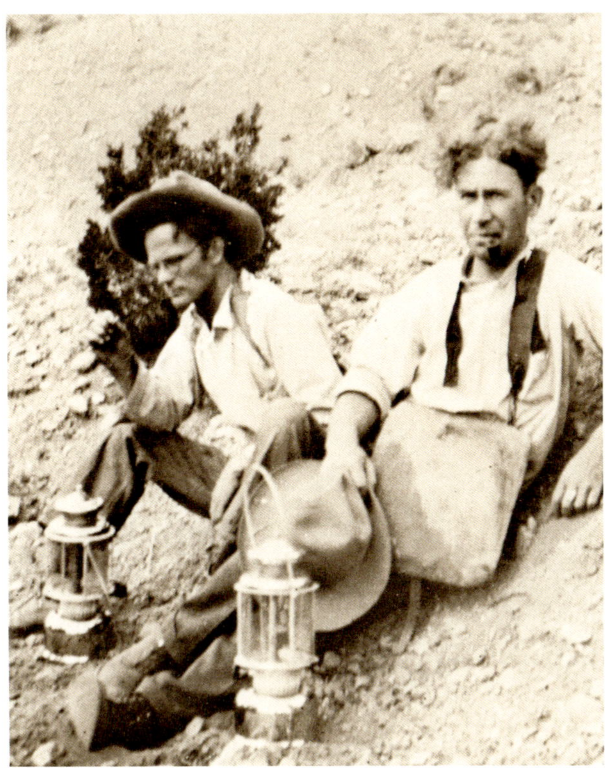

Will Shuster and Walter Mruk at the entrance to
Carlsbad Caverns, c. 1925

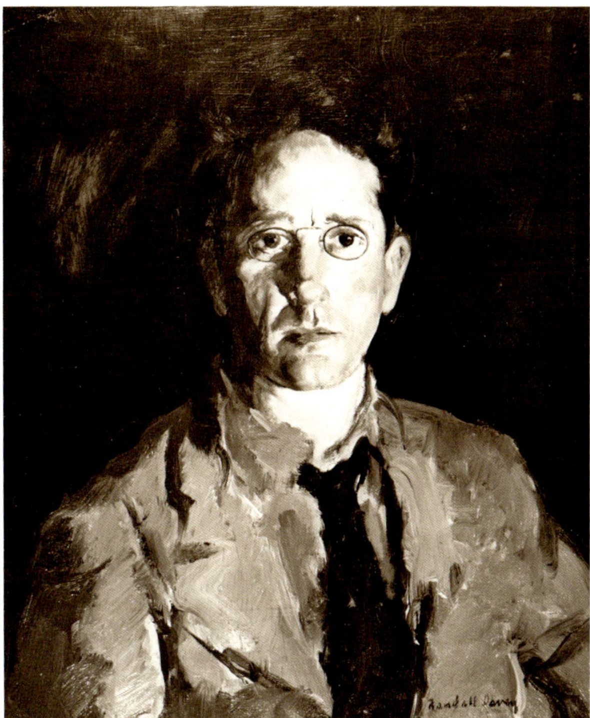

John Sloan, painted by Randall Davey, c. 1917

WILLIAM HOWARD SHUSTER (1893–1969)

A chronic lung ailment was not the only reason Philadelphian Will Shuster came to New Mexico: His mentor, John Sloan, had begun to summer in Santa Fe in 1919. Shuster followed in 1920, stopping first in Taos but soon settling in the capital after finding it full of artists—Henderson, Nordfeldt, Baumann, Vierra, Rush, Davey, and Cassidy, in addition to Sloan. A founding member of Los Cinco Pintores, he exhibited his paintings with the group and built his adobe house alongside theirs. During the 1920s Shuster experimented with abstraction, but his painting style remained essentially realist. Besides his oils, he is remembered for his Indian-theme murals at the Santa Fe Fine Arts Museum and for his robust etchings of life in the Southwest. And each September Santa Feans witness another Shuster creation: "Zozobra," or "Old Man Gloom," the giant puppet effigy burned annually to initiate the town's fiesta celebration.

JOHN SLOAN (1871–1951)

John Sloan, whose paintings were inspired by thirty summers in Santa Fe, played a pivotal role in the cultural growth of the town by promoting southwestern art in the East and influencing early exhibition policies at the Museum of New Mexico. Sloan's early experience as a Philadelphia newspaper illustrator was broadened by study with Thomas Anshutz and through association with Robert Henri and his circle in New York. There he participated in two famous exhibitions: the 1908 Macbeth Gallery show of The Eight and the Armory Show of 1913. Encouraged by his mentor and friend Henri, Sloan and his wife, Dolly, motored to Santa Fe in 1919 with the Randall Daveys. Returning annually, he painted genre scenes of the town and its environs. His palette, invigorated by the light and color of the Southwest, brightened considerably over the years.

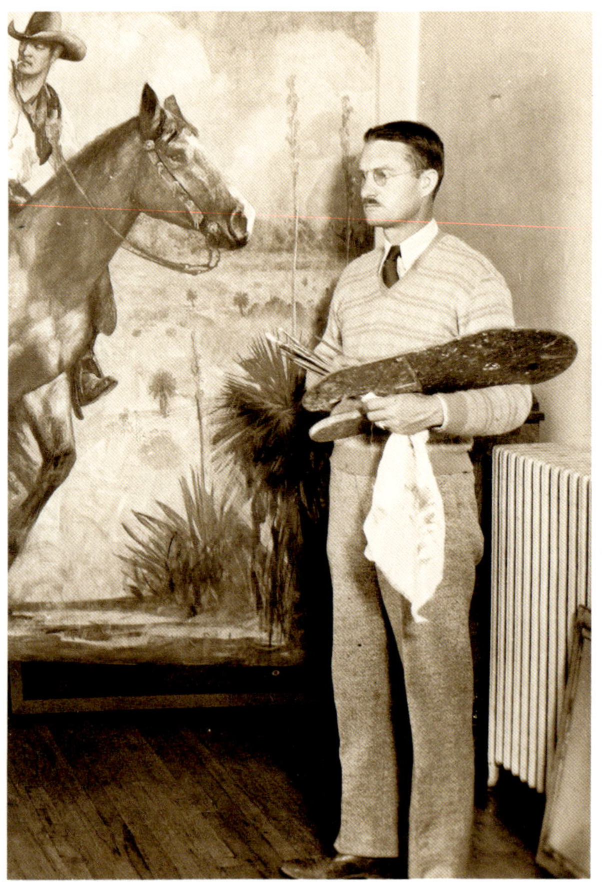

Theodore Van Soelen painting *Round-up*,
Santa Fe, c. 1935

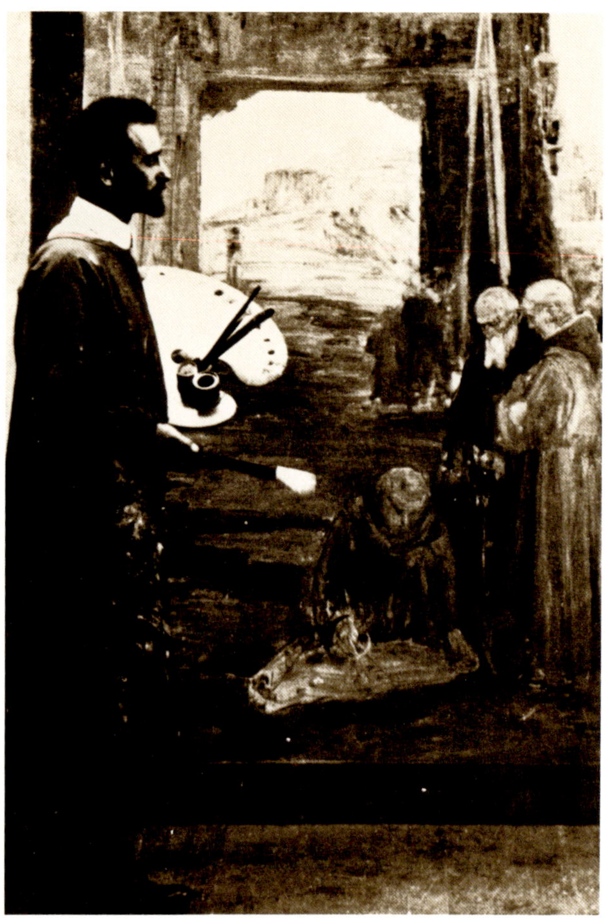

Carlos Vierra painting a mural for St. Francis
Auditorium, Fine Arts Museum, Santa Fe

THEODORE VAN SOELEN (1890–1964)

Van Soelen's early art training began in his hometown at
the St. Paul Institute of Arts and Sciences. Later he
earned a travel-study scholarship to Europe while at
the Pennsylvania Academy of the Fine Arts. In 1916
Van Soelen moved to Albuquerque to improve his
health. After four years illustrating and painting, he
wanted to observe Indian life more closely, so he moved
to a remote trading post. A later stay on a Texas ranch
offered the painter authentic insights into the life of
the working cowboy, another theme he pursued in
paint and lithography. Eventually he settled permanently at Tesuque, just outside Santa Fe, working as a
muralist for the Works Progress Administration and re-
cording the area and its people with a practiced, disciplined eye.

CARLOS VIERRA (1876–1937)

Vierra combined interests in painting, photography,
and archaeology to explore and record New Mexico architecture and landscape. A California native, he studied art and worked as a cartoonist in New York before a
lung ailment drove him to the Southwest. In 1904, he
became Santa Fe's first resident artist. Photography and
fieldwork lent authenticity to murals he painted in San
Diego and in the newly completed Fine Arts Museum
in Santa Fe. In careful paintings of the mission
churches at New Mexico's pueblos, Vierra lovingly recorded the blending of Pueblo and mission architecture
that became known as the "Santa Fe style," and that
could be seen in the home Vierra designed for himself
at the edge of town.

92

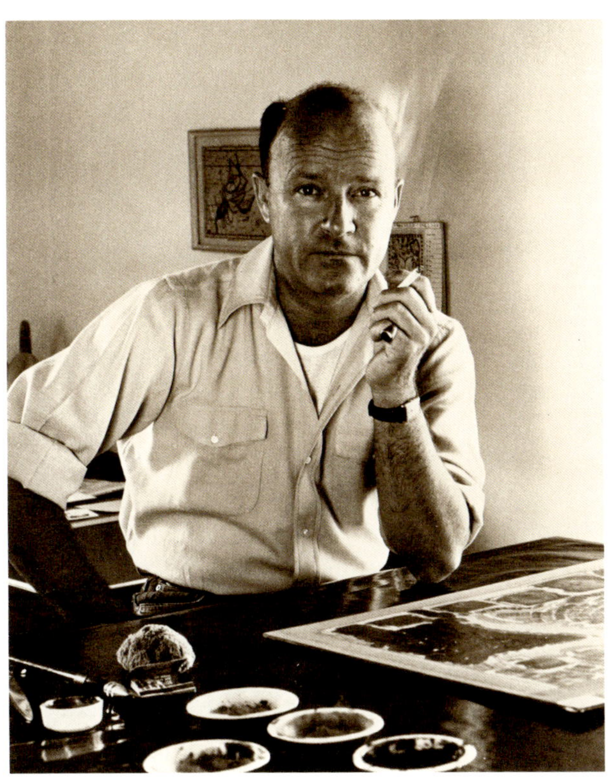

Cady Wells, c. 1947

CADY WELLS (1904–1954)

The son of an affluent eastern family, Wells moved to
Santa Fe in 1932 and studied painting with Andrew
Dasburg. Using watercolor, Wells transformed the New
Mexico landscape into dynamic brushstrokes on a
white background. He was fascinated by the region's
Hispanic culture and amassed a large collection of *san-
tos,* which he later gave to the Museum of New Mexico.
Influenced by Raymond Jonson and Georgia O'Keeffe
as well as by Dasburg, Wells responded distinctively to
a challenging topography.

❧ Bibliography ❧

Amon Carter Museum of Western Art. *Quiet Triumph: Forty Years with the Indian Arts Fund, Santa Fe*. Fort Worth, TX: Amon Carter Museum of Western Art, 1966.

Austin, Mary. *Red Earth*. Chicago, IL: Ralph Fletcher Seymour, 1920.

————. *The Land of Little Rain*. 1903. Reprint. Albuquerque, NM: University of New Mexico Press, 1974.

Balink, Henry C. Papers. Archives of American Art. Smithsonian Institution, Washington, D.C.

Ballinger, James K., and Andrea D. Rubinstein. *Visitors to Arizona, 1846 to 1980*. Phoenix, AZ: Phoenix Art Museum, 1980.

Barker, Ruth Laughlin. "John Sloan on Indian Tribal Arts." *Creative Art* 9 (December 1931): 445–49.

Baumann, Gustave, and Calla Hay. *Gustave Baumann*. Santa Fe, NM: Museum of New Mexico Press, 1972.

Bermingham, Peter. *The New Deal in the Southwest: Arizona and New Mexico*. Tucson, AZ: University of Arizona Museum of Art, 1980.

Breeskin, Adelyn D. *William Penhallow Henderson, 1877–1943: An Artist of Santa Fe*. Washington, D.C.: Smithsonian Institution Press, 1978.

Broder, Patricia. *The American West: The Modern Vision*. Boston, MA: New York Graphic Society, 1984.

Brooks, Van Wyck. *John Sloan: A Painter's Life*. London, England: J. M. Dent and Sons, 1955.

Bryant, Keith L., Jr. "The Atchison, Topeka and Santa Fe Railway and the Development of the Taos and Santa Fe Art Colonies." *Western Historical Quarterly* 9 (October 1978): 437–54.

Burlin, Paul. Papers. Archives of American Art. Smithsonian Institution, Washington, D.C.

Burnside, Wesley M. *Maynard Dixon: Artist of the West*. Provo, UT: Brigham Young University Press, 1974.

Cassidy, Ina Sizer. "Art and Artists of New Mexico: Andrew Dasburg and Theodore Van Soelen." *New Mexico Magazine* 10 (1932): 26, 40–41.

————. "Art and Artists of New Mexico: John Sloan and Gerald Cassidy." *New Mexico Magazine* 9 (1931): 31, 47.

————. "Art and Artists of New Mexico: Nordfeldt and Baumann." *New Mexico Magazine* 10 (1932): 24, 37.

————. "Art and Artists of New Mexico: Will Shuster." *New Mexico Magazine* 10 (1932): 18.

Chauvenet, Beatrice. *Hewett and Friends: A Biography of Santa Fe's Vibrant Era*. Santa Fe, NM: Museum of New Mexico Press, 1983.

Cikovsky, Nicolai, Jr. *Raymond Jonson: Pioneer Modernist of New Mexico*. New York: Berry-Hill Galleries, Inc., 1986.

Coke, Van Deren. *Andrew Dasburg*. Albuquerque, NM: University of New Mexico Press, 1979.

————. *Nordfeldt the Painter*. Albuquerque, NM: University of New Mexico Press, 1972.

————. *Taos and Santa Fe: The Artist's Environment, 1882–1942*. Albuquerque, NM: University of New Mexico Press, 1963.

————. "Why Artists Came to New Mexico: 'Nature Presents a New Face Each Moment.'" *Art News* 73 (June 1974): 22–23.

Cunningham, Elizabeth, with George Schriever. *Masterpieces of the American West: Selections from the Anschutz Collection*. Denver, CO: Anschutz Collection, 1983.

Dasburg, Andrew. Papers. Archives of American Art. Smithsonian Institution, Washington, D.C.

Davey, Randall. Papers. Archives of American Art. Smithsonian Institution, Washington, D.C.

Davis, Stuart. Papers. Archives of American Art. Smithsonian Institution, Washington, D.C.

DeKooning, Elaine. "New Mexico." *Art in America* 49, no. 4 (1961): 56–59.

Duncan, Kate C. *Cady Wells: A Retrospective Exhibition*. Albuquerque, NM: University of New Mexico, 1967.

Eldredge, Charles C., Julie Schimmel, and William H. Truettner. *Art in New Mexico, 1900–1945: Paths to Taos and Santa Fe*. New York: Abbeville Press, for National Museum of American Art, Smithsonian Institution, Washington, D.C., 1986.

Feldman, Sandra K. *William Penhallow Henderson, The Early Years: 1901–1916*. New York: Hirschl & Adler

Galleries, 1982.

Fox, Steve. "They Came to Find Health in the Sun." *The Santa Fe Reporter,* 1 May 1985, p. 15.

"Fremont Ellis." *El Palacio* 28, nos. 1–4 (1930): 16–17.

Garman, Ed. *The Art of Raymond Jonson, Painter.* Albuquerque, NM: University of New Mexico Press, 1976.

Garoffolo, Vincent. "The Woodblock Art of Gustave Baumann." In *New Mexico Artists, New Mexico Artist Series No. 3,* pp. 35–44. Albuquerque, NM: University of New Mexico Press, 1952.

Grand Central Art Galleries. *Memorial Exhibition, Julius Rolshoven.* New York: Grand Central Art Galleries, 1954.

Growdon, Marcia Cohn. *Artists in the American Desert.* Reno, NV: Sierra Nevada Museum of Art, 1980.

Harrison, Peter D. "Carlos Vierra: His Role and Influence on the Maya Image." *The Maya Image in the Western World.* Albuquerque, NM: University of New Mexico, 1986.

Hartley, Marsden. "Aesthetic Sincerity." *El Palacio* 5 (9 December 1918): 332–33.

————. "America as Landscape." *El Palacio* 5 (21 December 1918): 340–42.

————. "Red Man Ceremonials: An American Plea for American Esthetics." *Art and Archaeology* 9 (January 1920): 7–14.

————. "The Scientific Esthetic of the Redman." Parts 1, 2. *Art and Archaeology* 13 (March 1922): 113–19; 14 (September 1922): 137–39.

Haskell, Barbara. *Marsden Hartley.* New York: Whitney Museum of American Art, 1980.

Henri, Robert. *The Art Spirit.* Compiled by Margery Ryerson. Philadelphia, PA: J. B. Lippincott Co., 1960.

Hewett, Edgar L. "Recent Southwestern Art." *Art and Archaeology* 9 (January 1920): 30–48.

Homer Boss. Pine Bluff, AR: Southeast Arkansas Arts and Science Center, 1977.

Homer, William Innes, with Violet Organ. *Robert Henri and His Circle.* Ithaca, NY, and London, England: Cornell University Press, 1969.

Hoopes, Donelson F. "Randall Davey: The New York–Santa Fe Connection." *American Art and Antiques* (January–February 1979): 42–49.

Hunter, Russel Vernon. Papers. Archives of American Art. Smithsonian Institution, Washington, D.C.

Hunter, Sam. *B. J. O. Nordfeldt, An American Expressionist.* Pipersville, PA: Richard Stuart Gallery, 1984.

"In Memoriam: Gerald Cassidy." *El Palacio* 36 (11–18 April 1934): 121–24.

Jones, Byron B. "Henry Balink 1882–1963." *Southwest Art* 14 (October 1984): 88–97.

Jonson, Raymond. Papers. Archives of American Art. Smithsonian Institution, Washington, D.C.

Kraft, James, and Helen Farr Sloan. *John Sloan in Santa Fe.* Washington, D.C.: Smithsonian Institution, 1981.

Lane, John R. *Stuart Davis: Art and Art Theory.* Brooklyn, NY: Brooklyn Museum, 1978.

Levin, Gail. "Andrew Dasburg: Recollections of the Avant-Garde." *Arts* 52 (1977): 156–60.

Morang, Alfred. *Kiss the Sky for Me: Letters to Clair Latour.* Edited by William Ford. Santa Fe, NM: Antelope Press, 1959.

Mowbray-Clark, John. Papers. Archives of American Art. Smithsonian Institution, Washington, D.C.

Murray, Marion. "Art in the Southwest." *Southwest Review* 12 (1926): 281–93.

Museum of New Mexico. *Cady Wells 1904–1954.* Santa Fe, NM: Museum of New Mexico, School of American Research, 1956.

————. *Fiftieth Anniversary Exhibition.* Santa Fe, NM: Museum of New Mexico, Fine Arts Museum, 1967.

————. *Light and Color: Images from New Mexico.* Santa Fe, NM: Museum of New Mexico Press, 1981.

————. *New Mexican National Academicians.* Santa Fe, NM: Museum of New Mexico, 1964.

————. *Randall Davey: Artist/Bon Vivant.* Retrospective Exhibition. Santa Fe, NM: Museum of New Mexico, 1984.

————. *A Retrospective Exhibition of the Work of Van Soelen.* Santa Fe, NM: Museum of New Mexico, 1960.

Musick, Archie. *Musick Medley: Intimate Memories of a Rocky Mountain Art Colony.* Colorado Springs, CO: Jane and Archie Musick, 1971.

National Collection of Fine Arts. *Stuart Davis Memorial Exhibition.* Washington, D.C.: Smithsonian Institution Press, 1965.

"New Mexico Artists and Writers: A Celebration, 1940." Republication of 26 June 1940 Artists and Writers Edition of the *Santa Fe New Mexican*. Santa Fe, NM: Ancient City Press, 1982.

Nordfeldt, B. J. O. Papers. Archives of American Art. Smithsonian Institution, Washington, D.C.

Paul Burlin, Exhibition of Paintings and Drawings. Minneapolis, MN: University of Minnesota, 1949.

Pearce, Thomas Matthews. *Mary Hunter Austin*. New York: Twayne Publishers, 1965.

Perlman, Bernard B. *Robert Henri, Painter*. Wilmington, DE: Delaware Art Museum, 1984.

Pollock, Duncan. "Artists of Taos and Santa Fe: From Zane Grey to the Tide of Modernism." *Art News* 73 (January 1974): 13–21.

Reeve, Kay Aiken. *Santa Fe and Taos, 1898–1942: An American Cultural Center*. Southwestern Studies Monograph, no. 67. El Paso, TX: Texas Western Press, 1982.

Robertson, Edna. *Los Cinco Pintores*. Santa Fe, NM: Museum of New Mexico, 1975.

————. *Gerald Cassidy, 1869–1934*. Santa Fe, NM: Museum of New Mexico, 1977.

Robertson, Edna, and Sarah Nestor. *Artists of the Canyons and Caminos: Santa Fe, The Early Years*. Layton, UT: Peregrine Smith, 1976.

Roswell Museum and Art Center. *Willard Nash*. Roswell, NM: Roswell Museum and Art Center, 1979.

Russel Vernon Hunter, 1900–1955. Memorial Retrospective Exhibition. Santa Fe, NM: Roswell Museum and Museum of New Mexico Art Gallery, 1955.

Sandburg, Carl. *Complete Poems: Carl Sandburg*. New York: Harcourt Brace and Company, 1950.

Sandler, Irving. *Paul Burlin*. New York: American Federation of Arts, 1961.

Schwartz, Sanford. "When New York Went to New Mexico." In *The Art Presence*, pp. 85–94. New York: Horizon Press, 1976.

Scott, Evelyn. "Art Colonists Were Numerous, Active." *Wings* (October 1930), reprinted in the *Santa Fe New Mexican*, 12 November 1967, p. D2.

"'Shus' and Santa Fe: Man and Town — A Long Love Affair." *The Santa Fe New Mexican*, February 16, 1969, p. C2.

"Shuster Show to Bring Memories of Old Days." *Santa Fe New Mexican*, 26 December 1965, p. 6.

Spurlock, William Henry, II. "Federal Support for the Visual Arts in the State of New Mexico: 1933–1943." Master's thesis, University of New Mexico, 1974.

Starr, Kevin. "Painterly Poet, Poetic Painter: The Dual Art of Maynard Dixon." *California Historical Quarterly*, 56 (1977–78): 290–309.

Stevenson, Philip. "Santa Fe: A Study in Integrity." *New Mexico Quarterly* 3 (1933): 125–32.

Trenton, Patricia. *Picturesque Images from Taos and Santa Fe*. Denver, CO: Denver Art Museum, 1974.

Udall, Sharyn Rohlfsen. *Modernist Painting in New Mexico, 1913–1935*. Albuquerque, NM: University of New Mexico Press, 1984.

University of New Mexico Art Museum. *Andrew Dasburg*. Albuquerque, NM: University Art Museum, 1979.

————. *Raymond Jonson: A Retrospective Exhibition*. Albuquerque, NM: University Art Museum, 1964.

"Vierra Memorial Show." *El Palacio* 44, nos. 1–2 (5–12 January 1938): 10–12.

Walter, Paul A. F. "The Santa Fe/Taos Art Movement." *Art and Archaeology* 4 (December 1916): 330–38.

Weigle, Marta. "Publishing in Santa Fe, 1915–40." *El Palacio* 90 (Anniversary Issue, 1984): 10–19.

Weigle, Marta, and Kyle Fiore. *Santa Fe and Taos: The Writer's Era, 1916–1941*. Santa Fe, NM: Ancient City Press, 1982.

Wiggins, Walt. *Alfred Morang: A Neglected Master*. Roswell, NM: Pintores Press, 1979.

White, Robert R. "The New Mexico Painters, 1923–26." *Southwest Art* 15 (May 1986): 76–81.

William Penhallow Henderson: Master Colorist of Santa Fe. Phoenix AZ: Phoenix Art Museum, 1984.

Wynn, Dudley. "The Southwestern Regional Straddle." *New Mexico Quarterly* 5 (1935): 7–14.

Photographic Credits